Do-it-yourself

Employment Law

Melanie Hunt

LAW PACK™ GUIDE

Employment Law Guide
by Melanie Hunt

Published by
Law Pack Publishing Limited
10-16 Cole Street
London SE1 4YH
www.lawpack.co.uk

1st Edition 1997
2nd Edition 1998
3rd Edition 1999

© 1997-1999 Law Pack Publishing Limited
ISBN: 1-902646-24-X
All rights reserved.

Printed in Great Britain

Important facts

This Law Pack Guide contains the information, advice and example contracts and letters to help maintain employer/employee relations in line with the law and codes of practice. It is intended for use in England and Wales. However, much of the legislation is generally applicable, or is mirrored, in Scotland and Northern Ireland, but readers are advised that practices may vary in these jurisdictions.

The information this Guide contains has been carefully compiled from professional sources, but its accuracy is not guaranteed, as laws and regulations may change or be subject to differing interpretations.

Neither this nor any other publication can take the place of a solicitor on important legal matters. As with any legal matter, common sense should determine whether you need the assistance of a solicitor, rather than relying solely on the information in this Law Pack Guide.

Table of contents

How to use this Law Pack Guide

This Law Pack Guide can help you achieve a important legal objectives conveniently, efficiently and economically. Remember that it is important for you to use this Guide properly if you are to avoid later difficulties.

Step-by-step instructions for using this Guide:

1. Read this Guide carefully. If after thorough examination you decide that your requirements are not met by this Law Pack Guide, or you do not feel confident about completing your own documents, then consult a solicitor.

2. Each chapter of this Guide provides an overview of the background, current legislation and codes of practice relating to different areas of employment law which employers and employees ought to know about.

3. An employer is obliged to draw up and maintain certain employee records and to know about employment procedures. At the end of this Guide are Appendices containing example letters, an employment contract and notices. These are template documents, with important footnotes, for reference when drawing up your own. Employment-related procedure flowcharts are also included.

4. Always use pen or type on legal documents; never use pencil.

5. Employer and employee should keep signed copies.

6. Do not cross out or erase anything on your final documents.

7. Always keep legal documents in a safe place and in a location known to your company secretary and solicitor.

Introduction

Few legal fields change as rapidly as employment law. New statutes influenced by case law, economic policy changes, trade union practices, government intervention and the tremendous impact of membership of the European Union and the European Court of Justice all mean that employment law is constantly being tested, re-shaped and redefined. The last year in particular has seen a number of developments in the area of employees' rights. The changes in turn affect the relationship between employer and employee, and both parties need to be aware of their rights and duties. All employees have a right to know what law protects them in the workplace; and employers must know how changes in the law could affect their companies. The idea of seeking legal remedies through confrontation in the courts for violations of employment law has become increasingly acceptable in recent years.

One of the purposes of this book is to promote good communications in the workplace. It may draw your attention to areas of potential or actual conflict. When they arise, disputes can usually be resolved through deliberate, honest negotiation. No employer enjoys having to take disciplinary action – let alone dismiss an employee – because of the sense of failure it frequently brings on both sides. But if dismissal is the only course of action, it must be done in a legally acceptable way.

This Guide provides a broad overview of employment regulations, rights and duties for both employers and employees. It will alert you to the conditions, practices, responsibilities, duties and remedies that fall within the scope of employment law, and help you navigate your way through them.

Melanie Hunt

Recruitment

Recruitment is divided into two main sections in this chapter: the first on the legal requirements behind recruitment and the second, beginning on page 17, on recruitment guidelines and codes of good practice.

LEGAL REQUIREMENTS

When recruiting staff, it is very important that an employer complies with the legal requirements – in particular relating to discrimination – as laid down in legislation. The legal requirements that are dealt with in this chapter are:

- Discrimination
- Employee's past criminal convictions
- Employment of children under 16 years
- Restrictions on the employment of women
- Employment of EU & EEA nationals
- Employment of Non-EU nationals

Discrimination

This chapter deals with discrimination during the recruitment process. Chapter 5 takes a broader view of discrimination in employment, its definition and the legal recourse available to employees who feel they have been unlawfully discriminated against.

No matter whether employers are recruiting through employment agencies, job centres, careers offices or schools they have a duty not to discriminate. They must neither give instructions nor bring pressure to discriminate.

Discrimination on the ground of sex, race or marital status

It is unlawful for employers to advertise vacancies, select interview candidates or offer employment in a way that discriminates on the ground of sex, race or marital status. An employee or job applicant who feels that he or she has been discriminated against on any of these grounds can raise a complaint with the Equal Opportunities Commission, the Commission for Racial Equality or an employment tribunal.

Exceptions

There are some jobs for which the sex or race of the successful candidate may be a 'genuine occupational qualification' and in these circumstances discrimination in advertisements, in the interview procedure, in job offers, in offers of promotion, training or transfers is acceptable.

(a) **Sex**: A person's sex is a 'genuine occupational qualification' for a job in the following circumstances:

- where the essential nature of the job calls for someone of a certain sex for reason of **physiology** e.g. a female model;

- where it is necessary to preserve **decency or privacy** because the job is likely to involve physical contact with people of the opposite sex in circumstances where those people may reasonably object to the job holder being of the opposite sex, or because the holder of the job is likely to do work in the presence of people who are in a state of undress or are using sanitary facilities and therefore might reasonably object to the presence of a person of the opposite sex;

- where the nature or location of the job means that the job holder must **live in** the premises provided by the employer. Because it is impractical for them to live anywhere else and the premises are not equipped with separate sleeping accommodation or sanitary facilities for men and women, it is unreasonable to expect the employer to equip the premises with such accommodation or facilities;

- where the job is in a **single-sex establishment** or single-sex part of an establishment for people requiring special care, supervision or attention, and the essential character of that establishment or that part makes it reasonable to restrict the job to a person of the same sex as those for whom the establishment (or that part of it) exists;

- where the job is for the provision of **personal services** to people in order to promote their welfare, education or other similar services and those services can most effectively be provided by someone of a certain sex;

Highlight

There are some jobs for which the sex or race of the successful candidate may be a 'genuine occupational qualification'.

- where the job involves **working outside the UK** in a country whose laws and customs are such that the duties could not, or could not effectively be performed by a man (or by a woman);

- where the job is one of two held by a **married couple**.

(b) **Race**: A person's race is a 'genuine occupational qualification' for a job in the following circumstances:

- where the job involves **dramatic performance** and someone of a particular racial group is required for authenticity;

- where the job involves working as a **model** for producing works of art, picture or film and a person of a racial group is needed for authenticity;

- where the job involves working in a **restaurant** open to the public in a particular setting for which someone of a particular racial group is required for authenticity;

- where the job involves the provision of **personal services** to a particular racial group in order to promote their welfare and those services can be best provided by someone from the same racial group.

Age discrimination

There is no express legislation prohibiting discrimination on the ground of age, but there is a voluntary code of practice which attempts to tackle the problem of age discrimination. Also see chapter 5 on age discrimination as unlawful indirect discrimination.

Trade unions

It is unlawful for an employer to refuse employment on the grounds of membership or non-membership in a trade union.

Pregnancy

In relation to pregnancy, any decision not to appoint a woman on the grounds that she is pregnant is likely to be found to be discriminatory against sex.

Disability discrimination

It is unlawful for an employer with 15 or more employees to unjustifiably discriminate against a disabled person on the ground of their disability. This law applies in a similar way to the current sex and race legislation at all stages in the recruitment process. Employers with less than 15 employees are also encouraged to follow good practice guidelines.

Employee's past criminal convictions —

Spent convictions

After a certain period of time, people who have been convicted of criminal offences and who have served their sentences are not under a duty to disclose those convictions to a prospective employer. These convictions are known as 'spent' convictions. If spent convictions are disclosed to prospective employers it is unlawful for them to take the offences into account when considering someone for a job and if they do so they will be guilty of unlawful discrimination. The periods of time (known as rehabilitation periods) depend on the seriousness of the offence and are set out in Appendix 1. In certain professions, offices and occupations, all previous offences must be disclosed regardless of the period of time that has expired.

Unspent convictions

At present it is not legally possible to check the criminal records of potential employees because of restrictions imposed by data protection legislation. The Police Act contains a number of provisions to make available the criminal records of job applicants to employers. Under these provisions all job applicants will have to present a document, known as a 'criminal convictions certificate', disclosing any unspent convictions, if required to do so by an employer. The provisions are not yet in force but a Criminal Records Agency is due to be established to manage this information.

Employing children and young persons —

A 'child' is defined as anyone younger than the minimum school leaving age. 'Young persons' are defined as anyone over school leaving age but under 18. Young persons are protected by the terms of a European Directive on the Protection of Young People at work which were implemented into UK legislation within the Working Time Regulations which came into force on 1 October 1998.

No child may be employed:

- if under the age of 13 years;
- during school hours;
- before 7am or after 7pm;
- for more than two hours on any day on which he or she is required to attend school;

Highlight

After a certain period of time, people who have been convicted of criminal offences and who have served their sentences are not under a duty to disclose those convictions to a prospective employer.

- for more than two hours on a Sunday;

- in any industrial undertaking; or

- where they are likely to suffer injury from lifting, carrying or moving heavy items.

A local education authority has powers to supervise the employment of school children in its area and may require particulars about a child's employment. It may prohibit or restrict employment if it feels that the employment is unsuitable even if not unlawful. A person who wishes to employ a child must obtain a permit from the local education authority.

Restrictions on employing women

The following restrictions on the employment of women are for the protection of women and it is lawful to discriminate in employment to comply with these requirements:

- employment in factories within four weeks of child birth;

- employment in a range of processes involving lead or lead compounds;

- employment in a range of processes in the pottery industry;

- protection from exposure to ionising radiation; and

- employment on ships or aeroplanes while pregnant.

Employment of EU and EEA nationals

Highlight

EU nationals and nationals of member states of the European Economic Area do not need work permits. They have the right to come to the UK and look for work.

The 15 member States of the European Union (EU) are: Austria, Belgium, Denmark, Finland, France, Germany, Greece, Ireland, Italy, Luxembourg, the Netherlands, Portugal, Spain, Sweden and the United Kingdom. The European Economic Area (EEA) comprises EU members plus Iceland, Liechtenstein and Norway. Citizens of the EU and EEA are known as European Nationals and they do not need work permits; they have the right to come to the UK and look for work. Family members of European Nationals also have an automatic right to accompany such European Nationals to the UK. However, if they wish to stay in the UK for more than six months they are advised to apply for a residence permit.

Exception

Member States of the EU are entitled to exclude employment in public service from the general requirements of free movement of labour, and may reserve such employment for their own nationals. The definition of employment in public service in this context is not a question of status of the employee but rather on whether the employee exercises powers conferred by public law or is responsible for safeguarding the general interests of the state.

Employment of non-EU nationals

Someone who is subject to immigration control must obtain a work permit before taking up employment in the UK, unless he or she belongs to one of the categories of people for which this is not necessary. These include:

- ministers of religion;

- representatives of overseas newspapers, news agencies and broadcasting organisations;

- private servants of diplomatic staff;

- sole representatives of overseas firms;

- teachers and language assistants under approved exchange schemes;

- employees of an overseas government or international organisation;

- seamen under contract to join a ship in British waters;

- operational ground staff of overseas owned airlines;

- seasonal workers at agricultural camps under approved schemes;

- doctors and dentists in post-graduate training;

- business visitors admitted by the Home Office;

- Commonwealth citizens with the right of abode and those with at least one grandparent born in the UK.

For further details about applications for work permits contact The Department for Education and Employment Overseas, listed in Appendix 28.

The Asylum and Immigration Act has been introduced to discourage illegal working in the UK. This creates a new criminal offence (punishable by a fine of up to £5000) of employing a person without immigration authorisation to work in the UK and came into force on 27th January 1997. An employer will have a defence if it can prove that it saw an original of one of a number of specified documents which

Highlight

The Asylum and Immigration Act has been introduced to discourage illegal working in the UK.

confirmed that the employee was entitled to work in the UK (see Appendix 2). The Act is not retrospective so employers do not have to check documentation on staff employed prior to January 1997. It is important for employers to adopt procedures which will protect them from prosecution but which also do not breach the race discrimination legislation (see chapter 5). The Home Office has published guidance notes for employers which are available by telephoning 020 8649 7878.

RECRUITMENT GUIDELINES

Highlight

The Equal Opportunities Commission and the Commission for Racial Equality both publish codes of practice for employers.

As well as complying with employment legislation, employers are encouraged to follow good practice when recruiting. The Equal Opportunities Commission and the Commission for Racial Equality both publish codes of practice and recruitment guidelines for employers. Failure to observe these codes of practice does not render an employer liable to proceedings. But, if proceedings are brought in an employment tribunal under the Sex Discrimination Act 1975 or the Race Relations Act 1976, any relevant provision of either of the codes may be taken into account. Employers are advised to consider their practices carefully at each stage in the recruitment process. These are divided into:

- Advertising
- Selecting and interviewing job applicants
- Choosing the successful candidate
- Making the job offer

Advertising

Employers must avoid biased language in recruitment advertising. Adverts will be illegal if they discourage certain groups (as identified in the discrimination section of this chapter) from applying for the jobs. For example:

'Salesman wanted ...'.

This is an example of gender bias because the word "man" indicates that women applicants will not be considered for the position. The word "salesperson" would be acceptable, or alternatively an indication in the advertisement that both men and women may apply.

'Single professional sought ...'.

This is an example of discrimination on the grounds of marital status and is illegal because the employer is denying applications from qualified married people in favour of those who are unmarried.

In addition to the wording of the adverts, other points to consider, which the codes of practice referred to above recommend, are as follows:

- Always place adverts in publications or areas that are likely to reach both men and women and which do not exclude or disproportionately reduce the number of applicants of a particular racial group.

- Never present men and women in stereotyped roles.

- Be wary of recruiting solely by word of mouth as this may limit members of a certain sex or race from applying.

- If applicants are supplied through trade unions and members of only one sex or a particular racial group (or a disproportionately high number of them) come forward, discuss this with the unions; an alternative approach may have to be adopted.

- Never make the length of residence in or experience of the UK a requirement of the job.

- If a qualification for the job is required, always state that a fully comparable overseas qualification is as acceptable as a UK one.

What should an advertisement include?

It is good practice to prepare a written description for each job title. From this written description an employer may specify the most important duties and requirements of the vacant post in the advertisement as follows:

- the qualifications and experience required;

- any specific skills required;

- experience with specific equipment required;

- the salary and benefits offered;

- the person to contact;

- the required references.

If in doubt about whether the advert is appropriate, ask the personnel department, a legal adviser or someone in a senior position to review it before it is published.

Highlight

It is a good idea to include a statement in the advert that the employer is an equal opportunities employer.

Selecting and interviewing applicants ▬

Selection criteria and/or tests

The purpose of selection criteria and tests is to ensure that an individual has the ability to perform or train for a particular job. The employer should avoid insisting on irrelevant qualifications. Selection criteria and tests should be reviewed regularly to ensure that they remain relevant and are not unlawfully discriminatory.

Once selection of applicants has been carried out letters should be sent inviting candidates for interview and rejecting unsuccessful applicants (see the example letters at Appendices 3 and 4).

'Dos' and 'Don'ts' when selecting and interviewing job applicants

The following checklist outlines what the employer should and should not do during the selection and interview process:

<u>Do</u>

- process all applications in the same way

- ask questions at the interview which relate to the requirements of the job

- ensure that all employees who come into contact with job applicants are properly trained about legal obligations in respect of discrimination and how to avoid unlawful discrimination

- keep records of interviews showing why the applicants were or were not appointed

<u>Don't</u>

- keep separate lists of male and female or married and single applicants

- ask questions at the interview about personal circumstances such as marital status, children, domestic obligations, marriage plans or family intentions

- make jokes at the interview that are sexist or racist or otherwise biased

Highlight

Don't ask questions at the interview about personal circumstances such as marital status, children, domestic obligations, marriage plans or family intentions

Suggested questions for a job applicant to ask at an employment interview

An employer should provide basic information about the employment contract during the interview. If the employer does not provide information that answers the following questions, the applicant should ask:

1. What is the nature of the job? What are the duties and responsibilities?

2. What is the wage for the job? When and how are wages paid? If wages and bonuses are negotiable, they should be discussed during the interview (a fair employer should answer these questions; many recruitment agencies advise applicants to delay asking about salary and benefits until they have received a job offer; an employer's written job description often includes these details).

3. What are the hours of work? Starting times, break times and finishing times should be explained. Is overtime paid at a higher rate? Can it be made part of the employment contract?

4. What is the holiday entitlement? If an employee works on bank holidays, is it compensated by overtime pay or time off another day? Can unused holiday be carried over to the next year? Does an employee accrue holiday entitlement or holiday pay during maternity leave? Are employees paid accrued holiday pay if they leave the job?

5. What are the notice arrangements?

6. What are the sick-pay arrangements?

7. What about pensions?

8. What is the disclipinary and grievance procedure?

While reading this Guide, prospective employees should make a note of any other issues that seem important. Employers respect applicants who prepare for the interview in advance and ask clear, well-framed questions.

Making the job offer

After the selection process, and once a suitable candidate has been chosen, a conditional offer should be made. References should then be taken up and medical examinations should be arranged if required (see the example letters at Appendices 5 and 6). Once the preferred candidate has accepted the offer, rejection letters should be sent to the unsuccessful candidates (see the example letter at Appendix 7). Where a candidate accepts a job offer, but subsequently changes his or her mind (possibly opting for another offer), this technically may be breach of contract; unless the employer can prove financial loss as a direct result, there is little it can do.

Highlight

Once the preferred candidate has accepted the offer, rejection letters should be sent to the unsuccessful candidates.

Terms of employment

The contract of employment is the legal basis of the employee/employer relationship. This chapter outlines the main principles of employment contracts which employers need to know in order to avoid legal problems. Employees should also be aware of these so that they know their rights. The issues covered in this chapter are:

- General principles
- Employees and the self-employed
- Statutory rights of employees
- Types of contracts
- Terms of contracts
- Variation of contracts

General principles

A contract of employment is generally governed by the same legal principles as any other contract. in that there must be:

- an offer;
- an acceptance;
- valuable consideration;
- reasonable certainty in the terms; and
- an intention to create legal relations.

Highlight

The contract may be oral or in writing or a mixture of the two. However, employers have a duty to issue their employees a written statement of the main terms and conditions under which they are to be employed.

The contract may be oral or in writing or a mixture of the two. However, employers have a duty to issue their employees a written statement of the main terms and conditions under which they are to be employed. This must be issued within two months after the employment begins, but does not constitute the contract of employment. It is merely the employer's version of what he or she believes the main terms to be. The written statement may become a contract of employment but only where the parties have expressly agreed to this. A mere signature by the employee to acknowledge receipt of the written statement does not amount to agreement that the terms are the contract of employment.

In addition to the right to have a written statement issued, employees have further statutory rights, details of which are given on page 25. Subject to these statutory rights, the parties to a contract of employment are free to agree upon any terms they wish.

Employees and the self-employed

Any person who works for another person or organisation in return for remuneration has a contractual relationship with it. However, there is an extremely important distinction between an employee and a self-employed person, because their legal rights differ in a number of ways.

A *contract of employment* (sometimes referred to as a *contract of service*) is the name given to the agreement an employee has with an employer. A *contract for services* is the name given to the agreement between a self-employed person (or independent sub-contractor) and the person or organisation to whom he or she is providing the services.

To distinguish between a contract of employment and a contract for services it is necessary to look at the reality of the relationship, not merely the name of the agreement.

How to distinguish a contract of employment from a contract for services

Questions to consider in determining whether a person is an employee or is self-employed are:

1. Are there mutual obligations on the employer to provide work for the person engaged and on the person engaged to perform work for the employer?

2. Is he performing services for other people as a person in business on his own account?

3. Is he working under the orders of the person to whom he is supplying the services who controls when, how and what he must do?

4. Does he provide his own machinery and equipment?

5. Does he hire his own helpers?

6. Does he take a degree of financial risk?

Highlight

To distinguish between a contract of employment and a contract for services it is necessary to look at the reality of the relationship, not merely the name of the agreement.

7. Is the engagement for a specific, finite project or does it carry a degree of responsibility for ongoing administration or management?

8. Does he have the possibility of profiting from sound management in the performance of his tasks?

The greater degree of personal responsibility the person engaged undertakes in any of the above, the more likely he is to be considered self-employed rather than an employee. Other factors may include the method of payment, the method of paying tax and national insurance, payment during absence for illness or for holidays, membership of company pension schemes and a prohibition on working for other companies or individuals.

Although the above questions are relevant considerations, they will not be appropriate in every case and the answer to the question is not found by merely using these questions as a check list. It is important to assess each case individually.

Highlight
If there is any doubt as to the nature of the relationship the parties may agree on what the legal situation between them is to be.

If there is any doubt as to the nature of the relationship the parties may agree on what the legal situation between them is to be. However, it will not be conclusive when questions of tax, social security or statutory employment protection arise. If the matter goes to a court or tribunal all the circumstances will be considered to ascertain the true nature of the relationship.

To add to the confusion, some of the more recent legislation (such as the Working Time Regulations 1998 and the National Minimum Wage Act 1999) provides protection not just to 'employees' but to 'workers'. A worker includes both employees and others who provide services personally (although not under a client relationship) but does not include a person who is genuinely self-employed. This greatly increases the number of people protected by such legislation.

Practical and legal implications

Employees' statutory rights are dealt with separately in this chapter, but the following is a comparative list of the rights and obligations of employees and the self-employed.

Rights common to employees and the self-employed

- equal opportunities, i.e. non-discrimination on the grounds of race, sex or disability
- to be provided with a safe place of work and system of work
- to be paid wages or fees free of any deductions not properly authorised.

Rights limited to employees

- an itemised pay statement

- equal pay for equal work or work of equal value or work rated as equivalent

- maternity rights and benefits

- notice of termination of employment

- guaranteed pay

- redundancy pay

- reasonable care taken of his safety

- statutory sick pay

- remuneration on suspension on medical grounds

- time off for public duties, for trade union activities, duties and training, and to look for work if declared redundant with at least two years' service

- membership or non-membership of trade union and to take part in trade union activities

- protected employment rights where business is transferred to a new employer

- not to be unfairly dismissed

- written reasons for dismissal upon request

- a written statement of the terms and conditions of employment

- protection against dismissal or unfavourable treatment for taking certain actions on health and safety grounds

- protection against dismissal for asserting a statutory right

- to apply to an employment tribunal for a declaration that terms in a collective agreement or works rules are discriminatory on the grounds of sex

- to apply to the Secretary of State for payment of redundancy pay, pay arrears, notice, holiday pay, maternity pay, basic award or, reimbursement of fee or premium on insolvency of employer

- 3 weeks paid holiday rising to 4 weeks by November 1999, maximum working week of 48 hours, minimum breaks and rest period (not in force until approximately October 1998)

Highlight

Employees are entitled to a written statement of terms and conditions of employment.

Obligations of employees

- to obey the employer's lawful orders

- to work faithfully and with due diligence

- to give the contractually agreed or statutory minimum period of notice to terminate the employment

- to pay income tax by way of deductions under the PAYE scheme (which the employer must deduct)

- to pay employees' national insurance contributions (which the employer must make)

Obligations of self-employed

- to work with due skill and diligence

- to pay income tax under Schedule D

- to pay self-employed person's national insurance contributions

- to fulfil contractual obligations

Statutory rights of employees

Highlight
An employee becomes entitled to *statutory rights* upon entering into an employment contract.

An employee becomes entitled to *statutory rights* (i.e. laid down by law) upon entering into an employment contract. A number of these rights depend upon the employee having attained a qualifying period of employment. The main rights are described in more detail below.

1. *Equal opportunities* (see chapter 5)

2. *Itemised pay statements* An itemised pay statement must be issued to all employees at the time of payment and must include the following particulars:

   - gross earnings

   - net pay

   - fixed and variable deductions from gross earnings

   - if the net pay is paid in different ways, the amount and method of payment of each part payment

   Employees may raise a complaint with an employment tribunal if the employer fails to issue a pay statement or if the content is in dispute.

3. *Equal pay for like work or work rated as equivalent or work of equal value* (see chapter 5)

4. ***Maternity rights and benefits*** (see chapter 3)

5. ***Notice of termination of employment***

    Statute lays down minimum notice periods for termination of employment as follows:

    By the employer:

Length of service	Minimum notice period
Less than 1 month	Nil
1 month–2 years	1 week
2–3 years	2 weeks

    and an additional week for each year of continuous employment to a maximum of 12 weeks.

    By the employee: one week.

    The contract of employment may impose a duty to give a longer period of notice.

    See chapter 6 for further details on the recommended procedure for giving notice of termination of employment.

6. ***Guarantee pay***

    'Guarantee' payments must be made to employees with at least one month's service, when they could normally expect to work but no work is available. Periods when employees are laid off because there is no work available must be agreed in advance to avoid the employer being in breach of contract.

    An employee is entitled to a maximum payment of £15.35 per day for up to 5 days in any period of 3 months where they are laid off. Therefore, the annual maximum is currently £307. See Appendix 13 for an example notice to employees being laid off giving guarantee payments.

    An employee may raise a complaint with an employment tribunal if his or her employer fails to pay the whole or part of a guarantee payment to which he or she is entitled. The employment tribunal can award compensation equal to the amount of guarantee payment which it finds due to the employee.

7. ***Redundancy pay*** (see chapter 6)

Highlight
Guarantee payments must be made to employees with at least one month's service, when they could normally expect to work but no work is available.

8. *Healthy and safe working environment*

All employees are entitled to be provided by their employer 'so far as is reasonably practicable' with a safe place to work and access to the place of work, a safe system of work, adequate materials, competent fellow employees and protection from unnecessary risk of injury. Where there are more than five employees employed at any one time the employer must prepare and bring to the notice of its employees a written statement of its policy with respect to health and safety at work.

A model policy, intended for smaller businesses, is available from The Stationery Office but ideally the content of the policy statement should be tailored to meet the employer's particular requirements.

The Health and Safety at Work legislation is too complex to cover in this Guide, but employers should be aware of the importance of fulfilling their obligations. The Health and Safety Commission (HSC) and the Health and Safety Executive (HSE) are both established by the Health and Safety at Work etc Act 1974 and can provide advice. HSE publishes guidance notes on this subject which are available from HSE Books, listed at Appendix 30.

The Working Time Regulations provide for an average 48-hour working week; minimum breaks and 11 consecutive hours rest in any 24-hour period; three weeks paid holiday (rising to four weeks in November 1999) and an average 8 hours work in 24 hours for night workers.

9. *Sickness benefit* (See chapter 4)

10. *Remuneration on suspension on medical grounds*

Highlight
An employee is entitled to be paid for up to 26 weeks if he or she is suspended on medical grounds in compliance with any regulation or law which concerns the health and safety of workers.

An employee is entitled to be paid for up to 26 weeks if he or she is suspended on medical grounds in compliance with any regulation or law which concerns the health and safety of workers.

An employee is only entitled to claim a medical suspension payment if he or she has been continuously employed for a period of one month. An employee employed for a fixed term of three months or less or under a specific task contract which is not expected to last for more than three months is not entitled to a medical suspension payment.

An employee will lose the right to payment where:

*   he or she is incapable of work by reason of disease or bodily or mental disablement;

- the employer offered the employee suitable alternative employment (whether or not it was work that the employee was engaged to perform) and the employee unreasonably refused to perform that work; or

- he or she failed to comply with the employer's reasonable requirements imposed with a view to ensuring his or her services were available.

The amount an employee is entitled to be paid is 'a week's pay' (or a proportion of 'a week's pay') for every week of suspension. 'A week's pay' is calculated according to statutory rules and is also the basis for the calculation of redundancy payments and compensation for unfair dismissal.

Employees may raise a complaint with an employment tribunal for failure to make a medical suspension payment. Such a complaint must be made within three months of the day on which it is alleged that payment was not made. The tribunal will extend the time limit if it was not reasonably practicable for the claim to be made within three months.

11. *Time off*

(a) *Public duties*

An employee is entitled to time off for the purposes of performing his or her public duties; see Appendix 14 for a full list of such duties.

Time off is unpaid and the amount of time off depends upon the employer's business and the effect of the employee's absence.

There is no statutory right to have time off for jury service or attending court as a witness. However, an employer who prevents such attendance would be in contempt of court.

Although there is no legal obligation on employers to pay employees whilst they are on jury service, doing so is conducive to good employee relations. Jurors may however claim an allowance for travelling subsistence and financial loss.

(b) *Trade union activities, duties and training*

Officials of independent trade unions are entitled to time off with pay to perform duties concerned with the industrial relations in the company and to undergo training. (There will also soon be a right to time off to accompany another worker at disciplinary and grievance hearings.)

Highlight
There is no statutory right to have time off for jury service or attending court as a witness. However an employer who prevented such attendance would be in contempt of court.

Union members are entitled to time off without pay in order to take part in trade union activities.

(c) *Elected employee representatives*

An employee who has been elected for consultation purposes for collective redundancies or the transfer of an undertaking is entitled to reasonable paid time off to perform the functions of a representative. From 1 November 1999 they will also have the right to paid time off to undergo training.

(d) *Safety representatives*

Safety representatives who have been appointed by recognised trade unions are entitled to paid time off during working time to carry out their functions and undergo training in aspects of these functions. Representatives of non-unionised workplaces are also entitled to paid time off to carry out their functions and undergo training.

(e) *Pension scheme trustees*

Pension scheme trustees of the employers own scheme are entitled to time off during working hours for performing their duties of a trustee or for training in connection with those duties

(f) *Antenatal care*

See Chapter 3.

(g) *Redundancy*

An employee who is declared redundant and has at least 2 years' continuity of employment is entitled to reasonable, paid time off to look for a new job or to arrange training for a new job.

An employee may raise a complaint with an employment tribunal if the employer refuses to allow such time off or fails to pay for it.

12. *Protected rights on the transfer of a trade or business*

Highlight

Where a trade or business is transferred from one employer to another, the employees of that trade or business automatically become employees of the new employer, as if their contract of employment were originally made with the new employer

Where a trade or business is transferred from one employer to another, the employees of that trade or business automatically become employees of the new employer, as if their contract of employment were originally made with the new employer. The service is counted as continuous from the date on which the employment commenced with the first employer.

It is beyond the scope of this Guide to cover fully this complex area of employment law, and those who think they may be involved in a transfer of a trade or business should seek professional advice.

13. *Not to be unfairly dismissed* (see chapter 6)

14. *Written reasons for dismissal (upon request)*

An employee does not have an automatic right to a written statement of reasons for dismissal. However, if the employee has 1 years' continuous service and asks his or her employer for such a statement, the employer must provide one (the rules for assessing what is continuous service are set out in sections 210 to 219 of the Employment Rights Act 1996).

In practice, it is a good idea to give the dismissed employee the reasons for dismissal in the notice of termination.

15. *Written statement of terms and conditions of employment*

All employees have a right to be provided with a written statement of the terms and conditions of their employment unless (i) their employment is for a period of less than one month, (ii) they are engaged to work wholly or mainly outside Great Britain, or (iii) they are seamen. (Please note that the exceptions in (ii) and (iii) are due to be abolished by the Employment Relations Act 1999.)

The information that the employer provides may be given in installments but certain items must be given in a single document, described as the *principal statement* (see Appendix 9) Reference to other documents is permitted only in relation to certain limited matters. As already mentioned, the principal statement does not automatically constitute a contract of employment, even if the employee acknowledges receipt of it with his or her signature. To be enforceable, the parties must expressly agree that it is the contract of employment. It is quite usual for the particulars which constitute the written statement of terms and conditions to be incorporated into the contract of employment, because a separate document does not then have to be issued to the employee. The model contract of employment in this Guide at Appendix 10 incorporates all the particulars that must be included in the principal statement.

An employee employed for more than 13 weeks may raise a complaint with an employment tribunal if his or her employer fails to provide the written statement of the terms of employment. If a statement has been given but a question arises about particulars that should have been included in it, either employee or employer may apply to an employment tribunal.

Highlight
An employee employed for more than 13 weeks may raise a complaint with an employment tribunal if his or her employer fails to provide the written statement of the terms of employment.

16. *Parental leave*

From 15 December 1999 there will be a right for both men and women to take up to 13 weeks unpaid leave from work for the purpose of caring for a child for whom they have responsibility. For full details see chapter 3.

17. *Time off for domestic incidents*

There is also a new right (which also should be in force by the end of 1999) for employees to take a reasonable amount of unpaid leave to deal with incidents involving dependants. For full details see chapter 3.

18. *Minimum wage*

An employee's rate of pay must not be below the National Minimum Wage (NMW) which is currently £3.60 per hour before deductions for those aged 22 and above, £3.00 for those aged 18–21 and £3.20 for those in the first six months of a new job doing specific training. People aged 16 and 17, those on formal apprenticeships and those working and living as part of a family are not entitled to the NMW. Claims for NMW are heard in the employment tribunal.

Types of contracts of employment

There are a number of different types of contract of employment. When deciding which is the most appropriate, the employer should consider the type of work, the duration of the employment and the nature of the employment relationship that is sought by both parties.

Contract for an indefinite period

The majority of contracts of employment are for an indefinite period, as is the model contract included in this Guide (see Appendix 10). They can be terminated by either party giving notice. The period of notice should be specified in the contract, but if not there is an implied term (see page 34) that the contract may be terminated upon reasonable notice. In deciding what is reasonable, the following should be taken into account:

- seniority of the employee;
- remuneration of the employee;
- age of the employee;
- length of service of the employee;
- what is usual in the trade.

However, it is more advisable to express the notice period. To determine this employers should consider:

- How long is it likely to take to find a replacement for the employee if he or she resigns?

- Will a replacement need to be trained?

- How much would it cost to make a payment in lieu of notice? Long notice periods can be very costly.

- Is it possible that the employee will work for or become a competitor? In these circumstances a relatively long notice period is advisable.

- What is reasonable to expect from the employee?

- What is competitive in the market place?

The contractual notice period must not be less than the statutory minimum period of notice referred to on page 26 but if contractual notice is longer then the longer period must be given.

Fixed-term contracts

A fixed-term contract is one that has a termination date. The duration of the fixed-term contract may be for any period. Fixed-term contracts may provide that notice to terminate can be given before the termination date. If there is no notice provision, employment is guaranteed for the full period.

A fixed-term contract will automatically expire at the end of its term. Failure to renew a fixed-term contract upon termination may lead to a valid claim for unfair dismissal or redundancy pay (see page 83). However, currently unfair dismissal rights may be excluded in a contract for a fixed-term of one year or more and statutory redundancy payment rights may be excluded in a contract for a fixed-term of two years or more. The exclusion of these rights must be agreed upon in writing prior to the expiry of the term but this need not necessarily be contained in the contract of employment. Unfair dismissal and redundancy rights can only be excluded where dismissal consists of expiry of the term without it being renewed. Note however that the Employment Relations Act prohibits the waiver on unfair dismissal rights, but not on redundancy payment rights. (This provision is not yet in force but is likely to come into force by the end of 1999.)

Employers should be careful where fixed-term contracts are extended or renewed continually over long periods, and where they contain waiver clauses purporting to exclude the right to claim unfair dismissal and redundancy pay. There is some uncertainty as to whether a waiver clause

Highlight
The contractual notice period must not be less than the statutory minimum period

remains valid where an initial fixed-term contract of the requisite length (stated above) is extended for a shorter fixed term. The crucial distinction is between an extension or renewal of a contract on substantially the same terms, and re-engagement under a new fixed-term contract. In the first case the fixed term runs from the start of the original contract until the expiry of the extension, and any waiver clause will be valid. In the second case, there is a new fixed-term contract which must be for a term of at least one year in the case of unfair dismissal rights and two years in the case or redundancy rights if any waiver clause is to be effective.

Contracts for specific tasks

Contracts for the completion of a specific task are not fixed-term contracts but will automatically terminate once the task is completed.

Short-term contracts

These can be used where the work to be done can be completed within a short period of time. Where the contract is for less than three months the employee is not entitled to statutory sick pay or medical suspension pay. However, if a second such contract is entered into with the same employer and it is continuous with the first then the employer becomes liable to pay statutory sick pay or medical suspension pay.

Service contracts

This is the name given to a contract of employment for more senior employees. Service contracts may be fixed-term contracts renewable on a regular basis or they may be 'rolling' service contracts, in which the contract continues after the expiry of a fixed period and then can only be terminated by not less than, say, one year's notice.

Although service contracts can be expensive for a company they offer a measure of security and so are attractive for employees.

Directors may not have service contracts for more than five years without the agreement of the shareholders of the company at a general meeting.

Terms of contract ▬▬▬▬▬▬▬

1. *Express and implied terms*

Usually, the parties to the contract will have expressly stated the major terms of the contract. These may be written or oral but it is obviously preferable to put these terms in writing in order to minimise future disputes. Even though in practice express, oral terms may be just as binding as written ones they are very much more difficult to prove.

In addition to the express terms of the contract, all contracts of employment have what is known as 'implied terms'.

Implied terms are not stated expressly in the contract because:

*   they are too obvious to be recorded; or

*   they are common practice within the particular business or industry and are precise, reasonable and well known; or

*   they are necessary to make the contract work; or

*   the parties to the contract have shown by their behaviour their acceptance of such terms.

A term is not implied simply because it would be reasonable to include it. There are terms which are accepted as commonly implied in employment contracts relating to the employer's and the employee's duties, as shown in the table below.

Common Implied Terms

Employer's Duties

*   to pay **wages** (see below)

*   to **co-operate** with the employee and maintain mutual trust and confidence

*   to take reasonable care for the **health and safety** of the employee

*   to take reasonable steps to bring to the employee's attention any **contractual rights** which are dependent on them taking action, but which the employee may be reasonably unaware of

*   to exercise **pension rights** in good faith

*   to deal reasonably and promptly with **employees' grievances**

*   to give a reasonable period of **notice of termination** when no specific period of notice has been agreed

Employee's Duties

- to work for the employer with due **diligence and care**

- to **co-operate** with the employer, including obeying lawful orders, and maintain trust and confidence and not impeding the employer's business

- to follow a duty of **fidelity** i.e. not compete with the employer and not disclose confidential information unless in the public interest

- to take reasonable care for their own **safety** and that of fellow employees

- to give a reasonable period of **notice of termination** when no specific period of notice has been agreed

In addition to those in the table above, terms may be implied into a contract of employment by legislation, for example equality clauses which are implied by the Equal Pay Act 1970; these terms automatically apply to any contract.

Terms may also be incorporated into a contract of employment from other sources. Prime examples are terms which may be implied into an individual contract through collective agreements and work rules or staff handbooks.

2. *Unenforceable terms*

(a) *Unlawful terms or terms contrary to public policy*

For example, a contract which has the effect of being a fraud on the Inland Revenue or a contract under which a foreign employee works illegally without a work permit.

(b) *Terms purporting to contract out of employment protection legislation*

(c) *Discriminatory terms*

For example, on the grounds of sex, race or disability.

(d) *Terms in restraint of trade if their main purpose is to restrain competition*

Such terms *are* enforceable, however, if their main purpose is to protect something in which the employer has a legitimate business interest worthy of protection. For any such clause to be enforceable it needs to be carefully drafted, taking into account the nature of the employee's work. If the clause is too wide it will be void. The courts will not rewrite clauses to make them enforceable; an example of a restraint of trade clause is given at clause 10 at Appendix 10

(e) *Terms which purport to exclude or restrict liability for death or personal injury resulting from negligence*

In the case of loss or damage other than death or personal injury a contract term may only exclude or restrict liability for negligence if it satisfies the requirement of reasonableness (for further details on this see the Unfair Contract Terms Act 1977).

Variation of contract

An employer does not have an automatic right to vary an employee's terms of employment. The extent to which employers can unilaterally change an employee's terms or working arrangements will depend entirely on the terms themselves.

Existing terms

Flexibility may be expressly built into the contract by, for example, the inclusion of wide terms or narrow, but changeable terms. An example of the former is 'You may be required to work anywhere in the UK' while an example of the latter is 'You will work 8 hours in 24, day, night or shift work'. Another way flexibility may have been built into the contract is by the use of terms which can be altered in content or removed. For example, a bonus may be stated to be payable at the manager's discretion.

The contract may also contain what is known as 'machinery for change'. For example, the staff handbook 'as issued from time to time' may be stated to be incorporated. This would mean that matters dealt with in the handbook could be changed and the change incorporated into the contract, without the need of the employee's express consent.

If the contract contains such flexible clauses or incorporates machinery for change then the employer will be able to alter the terms in line with these clauses.

If there is no flexibility or machinery for change then employers must follow the correct procedure if they want to alter an employee's terms of employment, in order to minimise the possibility of claims for damages and/or compensation relating to the change.

Offering new terms to the employee

The first step for the employer is to offer the new terms to the employee. He can either accept or reject them. Acceptance must be positive, unequivocal and unconditional. There is no particular form of offering or acceptance required, so it can be oral, written or by conduct.

Highlight

An employer does not have an automatic right to vary an employee's terms of employment.

Appendix 15 provides an example letter from an employer to an employee altering the terms of employment. However, by doing nothing an employee cannot be said to have accepted the new terms. The only time doing nothing can amount to acceptance is when the contract contains a term making this so. An example of such a term would be, 'If you do not object in writing within 14 days you will be deemed to have accepted the change'. It is possible for an employee to accept the new terms by his conduct: if he changes his behaviour to comply with a term in the offer (for example he turns up for work at a new time) he will be taken to have accepted the new terms.

Dismiss and offer employment on new terms

If the employee does not accept the changes the only other option for the employer is to dismiss him and offer employment on the new terms. However, by doing this the employer may become liable for claims for breach of contract, unfair dismissal or redundancy if the correct procedures are not followed and the appropriate reasons for dismissal do not exist. Termination of employment is dealt with in greater detail in chapter 6 but if employers wish to take this route it is suggested that they take advice before doing so.

Family-
friendly rights

Employees have some important statutory rights in relation to their family responsibilities (subject to them satisfying certain qualifying conditions), which aim to strike balance between their work and home commitments. This chapter describes the various rights and is divided into sections as follows:

- Maternity rights

- Parental leave

- Time off for dependants.

Please note however that the law in this area is currently under going some significant changes, and at the time of writing some of the changes in the law have yet to come into force and this has been indicated in the text.

Maternity rights

The main statutory rights that a female employee who is expecting a baby has are explained in this chapter and are as follows:

- Time off for antenatal care

- Protection from dismissal and detrimental treatment

- Suspension from work on maternity grounds

- The right to take maternity leave and return to work

- Statutory maternity pay

Time off for antenatal care

Highlight

All pregnant employees are entitled to paid time off for antenatal care irrespective of their length of service or the number of hours worked by them.

All pregnant employees are entitled to paid time off for antenatal care, irrespective of their length of service or the number of hours worked by them. This right applies only to pregnant women; husbands of pregnant women have no statutory right to attend antenatal appointments with their wives.

Except in the case of the first appointment, the employee must produce a certificate confirming her pregnancy and an appointment card or some other document showing that an appointment has been made, if requested to do so by her employer.

The actual length of absence for antenatal care must be reasonable. It may include time for travelling to and from an appointment. If an appointment lasts longer than expected, the employer should still be obliged to pay the employee for the whole of the time that was required to attend the appointment. However, employees must not abuse their right by taking more time off than is necessary.

It may be reasonable for an employer to refuse an employee time off. Such refusal is reasonable in the circumstances that the employee can arrange to have the antenatal care outside normal working hours. Therefore, part-time staff or shift workers may be able to arrange appointments outside their normal working hours. However, the timing of appointments is often outside the individual's control and, if this is so, the employee should explain this to her employer. In these circumstances, it would be unreasonable for the employer to refuse the employee time off for antenatal care during her working hours. An employer cannot require an employee who takes time off for antenatal care to make up the time later.

What care is included in the right?

Statute does not define antenatal care except that it must be on the advice of a registered medical practitioner, midwife or health visitor. As a general guideline, however, it should be assumed that standard antenatal clinic visits are covered. The number of visits required and the length of each visit depends on the medical condition of the employee concerned.

An employment tribunal has held that exercise and relaxation classes also fall within the definition of antenatal care. But such classes would have to be on the recommendation of the employee's medical advisers.

There is no right to be paid for time off for infertility treatment. However, if an individual receiving infertility treatment becomes pregnant, then she enjoys the same statutory protection as any other pregnant employee. It is likely that she would need more time off work for antenatal care and an employer would be obliged to allow her the time off as it would probably be considered reasonable.

Doctors' appointments for the purpose of ascertaining whether or not an employee is pregnant would probably be regarded as antenatal care if the employee turned out to be pregnant but, if the employee were told that she was not pregnant, she would not be covered by the statutory right.

Highlight
An employment tribunal has held that exercise and relaxation classes also fall within the definition of antenatal care.

Pay entitlement

The employee should be paid her normal hourly rate of pay by her employer during the period of time off. If the employee is paid on the basis of a fixed salary, she should be paid as usual. Where an employee is paid by the hours she works, the rate of pay is calculated by dividing the amount of one week's pay by the normal working hours in a week.

If the number of hours worked per week is irregular, they should be averaged over the previous 12 complete working weeks. If the employee has not been employed for 12 weeks, the average should be calculated on the number of normal working hours in a week which she could reasonably expect to work under her contract of employment, or from the number of hours worked by any fellow employees in comparable employment.

Some employees may have a contractual right to be paid for time off for antenatal care. There is no right to receive both the contractual pay and the statutory pay and such entitlements can be offset against each other.

Remedies

If an employee is unreasonably refused time off, she would be guilty of misconduct if she took the time off without authorisation. However, an employee may raise a complaint with an employment tribunal if:

- her employer unreasonably refuses to give her time off for antenatal care; or

- her employer fails to pay her the appropriate amount for the time taken off for the antenatal appointment.

If a complaint is upheld, the tribunal will make a declaration to that effect. Where the complaint is a refusal to allow time off, the tribunal will order that the employer pay the employee the amount of remuneration to which she would have been entitled had time off been allowed. Where the complaint is a failure to pay the whole or part of the amount due, the tribunal will order that the employer pay the amount due.

If an employer unreasonably refuses to allow an employee time off for antenatal care and she has at least one year's service, she may also claim constructive dismissal in an employment tribunal. It is automatically unfair to dismiss a woman on the ground that she took proceedings to enforce her right to time off for antenatal care or allege that such right had been infringed.

Highlight
If an employer unreasonably refuses to allow an employee time off for antenatal care and she has at least two years' service, she may also claim constructive dismissal in an employment tribunal.

Exceptions

The only exceptions are women who are generally excluded from the maternity protection provisions which include share fisherman and women who ordinarily work outside Great Britain. (Please note that these exceptions are due to be abolished by the Employment Relations Act 1999.)

The right to time off for antenatal care should not be confused with time off for sickness during pregnancy.

Protection from dismissal and detrimental treatment

Dismissal or selection for redundancy of any woman who is pregnant, or has recently given birth, is automatically unfair regardless of her length of service or hours of work, if any of the following apply:

- The reason or principal reason for dismissal is that she is pregnant or any other reason connected with her pregnancy.

- Her maternity leave period (as defined below) is ended by her dismissal and the reason or principal reason for her dismissal is that she has given birth to a child, or any other reason connected with her having given birth to a child.

- The reason or principal reason for her dismissal, where her contract of employment was terminated at the end of her maternity leave period, is that she took, or otherwise availed herself of the benefits of maternity leave.

- The reason or principal reason for her dismissal is a requirement or recommendation to suspend her on health and safety grounds.

- The reason or principal reason for her dismissal is that she has given birth to a child, or any other reason connected with her having given birth to a child, and her contract of employment was terminated within four weeks of the end of the maternity leave period. The circumstances of termination were such that she remained incapable of work by reason of disease or other disablement and there was in force at that time, a certificate from a medical practitioner issued during the maternity leave period.

- The reason or principal reason for her dismissal is that she is redundant and her employer has not offered her suitable available alternative employment.

For further details on unfair dismissals and the remedies available for unfair dismissal see chapter 6, *Termination of employment*.

A dismissal by reason of pregnancy may also amount to direct discrimination on the grounds of sex (see chapter 5, *Discrimination*). From 15 December 1999 there will also be a new right not to be subject to detrimental treatment on grounds of pregnancy, childbirth or maternity. Employees may seek redress through an employment tribunal for infringement of this right.

An employee who is dismissed at any time during her pregnancy or maternity period is entitled to written reasons for her dismissal, regardless of length of service, without having to make a request for written reasons. An employee may raise a complaint with an employment tribunal if she is not provided with written reasons for her dismissal. If the employment tribunal finds the employer has breached this obligation unreasonably, it may make a declaration as to what it finds the employer's reasons for dismissal to have been. The employment tribunal may also award the employee a sum equivalent to two weeks' pay.

Suspension from work on maternity grounds

Under health and safety at work legislation employers have an obligation to carry out risk assessments for the safety of employees. This assessment must include any risk posed to the health and safety of a woman who is of childbearing age.

If the assessment shows that there is a risk to an employee, the employer has an obligation to take preventative or protective action. The employer may need to vary the employee's working conditions or hours of work. If this would not be reasonable or would not avoid the risk, the employee has a right to be offered any suitable alternative work which is available. If no suitable alternative work is available, the employer has a duty to suspend the employee from work for as long as necessary to avoid the risk. The employee has these rights regardless of length of service or number of hours that she works. However, to be entitled to these rights the employee must notify her employer in writing that she is pregnant, has given birth within the previous six months or is breastfeeding. Sick notes giving an indication of pregnancy may amount to written notification for these purposes.

Right to suitable alternative work

Alternative work is only suitable if it is both convenient and appropriate for the employee in question and is on terms and conditions no less favourable than her normal terms and conditions.

If suitable alternative work is available but the employer fails to offer it to the employee, the employee may raise a complaint with an employment tribunal, which may award compensation.

If the employer makes an offer of suitable alternative work but the employee unreasonably refuses the offer, she loses her right to be paid remuneration for the period of suspension (as described below).

Remuneration during suspension

If an employee is suspended on maternity grounds she is entitled to full pay during the period of her suspension (subject to above). In addition to the statutory right, an employee may have a *contractual* right to remuneration during maternity suspension. In these circumstances such entitlements should be offset against each other.

During the period of maternity suspension an employee retains her continuity of employment.

If an employer fails to pay an employee all or part of any money due, the employee may raise a complaint with an employment tribunal, which will award her the amount of remuneration that it finds due.

The right to take maternity leave and return to work

All employees who are expecting a baby are entitled to 14 weeks' maternity leave, regardless of their length of service or hours of work. This increases to 18 weeks from 15 December 1999. Employees who are expecting a baby and have two years' (reducing to one year from 15 December 1999) continuous service with their employer by the 11th week before the expected week of childbirth are entitled to extended maternity absence of up to 29 weeks, beginning with the week the child is born. Employees who have taken maternity leave or maternity absence normally have the right to return to the same job.

These rights to maternity leave and maternity absence apply where a woman gives birth to a living child or has a still birth after 24 weeks of pregnancy.

Highlight
Employees who have taken maternity leave or maternity absence normally have the right to return to the same job.

Maternity leave (to be renamed 'Ordinary Maternity Leave')

(i)   *Duration*

Maternity leave may not commence before the start of the 11th week before the beginning of the week in which the baby is due. Subject to this, maternity leave begins on the date the employee tells her employer she intends her leave to start. However, maternity leave can begin earlier than the date the employee chooses if she is absent from work for a reason which is wholly or partly because of her pregnancy. The Department of Social Security publishes a free leaflet *Pregnancy related illnesses*, NI200, which sets out the illnesses which are recognised as being connected to pregnancy. In these circumstances, her maternity leave shall begin on the first day of her absence, provided that date is after the beginning of the sixth week before the start of the week the baby is due.

In most circumstances maternity leave ends 14 weeks (soon to be 18) after it begins. However, women are prohibited from working within two weeks of childbirth. If a child is born later than expected and the two weeks following childbirth do not fall within the 14 (or 18)-week maternity leave period, then the period may be extended by up to two weeks. It is a criminal offence for an employer to fail to comply with this prohibition.

(ii)   *Notification*

Currently an employee is only entitled to maternity leave if she gives the required notice in writing (note that from 15 December 1999, verbal notice will suffice) of:

- the fact that she is pregnant;

- the expected week her baby is due (or the date of the birth in the unlikely event that it has already occurred); and

- the date she wishes her leave to begin.

Notification must be given at least 21 days before the maternity leave period commences or, if that is not possible, as soon as is reasonably practicable thereafter. In addition to compulsory notification and if the employer so requests, the employee must produce a certificate from a registered medical practitioner or midwife stating the expected week the baby is due.

If the maternity leave period has started before the notified leave date, either due to pregnancy-related absence or the employee

Highlight

In most circumstances maternity leave ends 14 (soon to be 18) weeks after it begins. However, women are prohibited from working within two weeks of childbirth.

giving birth, the employee must notify her employer as soon as she can that she is absent for whatever reason. If the employer requests, this notification must be in writing.

(iii) *Rights during maternity leave*

During maternity leave an employee is entitled to all the benefits that she would have received had she not been on maternity leave, except remuneration. This means that the contract of employment continues and the period on maternity leave counts towards her continuity of employment.

(iv) *Contractual rights*

It is not uncommon for an employee's employment contract to grant more favourable maternity provisions than the statutory rights.

Maternity absence (to be renamed 'additional maternity leave')

(i) *Duration*

Maternity absence may last up to 40 weeks (11 weeks before the expected week of childbirth and 29 weeks after the actual week of birth).

(ii) *Notification*

Currently the employee must meet the same notification requirements as for her maternity leave. However, if she wants to return to work after maternity absence she must state this in her notice to her employer. From 15 December 1999 no notice needs to be given by the employee of her intentions to take additional maternity leave. It is presumed she will take it unless she notifies otherwise.

(iii) *Rights during maternity absence*

Currently the employment status of a woman taking maternity absence is unclear. The Government has proposed to clarify this uncertainty. From 15 December 1999 it is proposed that the contract of employment continues during the additional maternity leave period but the only terms and conditions that need apply will be the employers obligations of trust and confidence and the employees obligations of good faith.

Right to return to work

(i) *Maternity leave (to be renamed 'ordinary maternity leave')*

An employee returning after 14 (or 18) weeks' maternity leave normally has the right to return to the same job that she left. If she wants to return to work before the end of her 14 (or 18)-week leave she must give her employer at least seven days' notice (due to be extended to 21 days from 15 December 1999) of the date she intends to return to work.

(ii) *Maternity absence (to be renamed 'additional maternity leave')*

An employee returning after maternity absence has the right to return to work of the same nature, capacity and location, at the rate of pay which she would have received had she not been absent at all, and on terms and conditions which are no less favourable than those which would have applied had she not been absent from work after the end of her maternity absence.

There are circumstances when the employer may offer suitable and appropriate alternative work if it is not reasonably practicable to allow the employee to return to work.

An employee who wishes to return to work after maternity absence must give her employer 21 days' notice of her intended date of return.

The employer may write to the employee asking for confirmation of the employee's intention to return to work (see example letter Appendix 16). This letter must be sent no earlier than 11 weeks after the employee's expected week of childbirth and no later than 21 days before her due date of return. If the employee does not reply to this letter within 14 days she loses her right to return to work. She has the right to change her mind at this late stage but if her answer is no, she has no right to change her mind. From 15 December 1999 these notification requirements change so that where the employee has not been in touch to notify the date of the birth, the employer may write no earlier than 21 days before the end of the ordinary maternity leave seeking confirmation of the date of birth and her intention to return. The employee must respond within 21 days of receiving the request. Where the employee fails to respond, she does not lose her right to return to work but the employer can take appropriate disciplinary action.

If the employer refuses to allow a woman to return from maternity leave she will be entitled to claim unfair dismissal. Recent case law would suggest a claim of sex discrimination may also be successful in these circumstances.

Employees who have taken maternity leave or maternity absence are increasingly likely to ask to return on a part-time basis. For both types of leave the entitlement is actually to return to the job she left, i.e. a full-time one. However, the employer must consider such requests carefully. If a part-time job is not a viable option, a

Highlight
Employees who have taken maternity leave or maternity absence are increasingly likely to ask to return on a part-time basis.

full explanation must be given showing grounds on which refusal can be justified. An unjustifiable refusal to offer part-time work can result in a successful claim of indirect sex discrimination, on the basis that the requirement to work full-time is one that fewer women than men can comply with because of family responsibilities.

Currently the date of the employee's return to work may be postponed by up to four weeks by the employer for any specified reason and by the employee if she is unfit to return to work and she provides a medical certificate. If the employee remains sick at the end of the four-week postponement recent case law states that the right to return is not necessarily lost. Therefore, a hasty termination of the contract could lead to claims of unfair dismissal and sex discrimination. However, from 15 December 1999 there is no right for the employee to postpone the return to work after additional maternity leave. If the employee is sick, the normal company rules on sick leave will apply.

Statutory maternity pay ═══════════════

Statutory maternity pay (SMP) is a payment that employers are required to make to eligible employees, even if the employee does not intend to return to work after the child is born.

Eligibility

An employee only qualifies for SMP if:

- she has stopped work wholly or partly because of pregnancy or childbirth; and

- she has 6 months' continuous employment with the same employer by the start of the 14th week before the expected week of childbirth; and

- her normal weekly earnings in the eight weeks before the start of the 14th week before the expected week of childbirth were above the lower earnings limit for the payment of National Insurance contributions, currently £66 (if the employee's normal weekly earnings are below the lower earnings limit, she can apply for maternity allowance from the DSS on Form SMP1); and

- she has reached the start of the 11th week before the expected week of childbirth (or if before, she has given birth).

Entitlement

The employee is entitled to SMP for 18 weeks (known as the 'maternity pay period') as follows:

- for the first six weeks, 90% of her normal weekly earnings;

- for the rest of the maternity pay period, a flat rate currently of £59.55 per week.

SMP is subject to income tax, National Insurance contributions and any other regular deductions and should be paid by the same method and at the same time as the employee would normally be paid. If there is no normal agreement as to which day wages are paid on, payment should be made on the last day of the calendar month.

The employee may also have a contractual right to maternity pay which the employer may set off against SMP.

How to make a claim for SMP

To make a claim, the employee simply gives her employer 21 days' notification that she will be absent because of her pregnancy or as much notice as is practicable. The employer may request this notice be in writing and then is obliged to complete various forms. The Government-run Employer's Helpline can provide further details on 0345 143143.

If the employee gives birth before the date notified or before the 14th week before the expected week of childbirth, she must give notice stating that her absence is due to the birth, within 21 days of the birth, or as soon as is reasonably practicable thereafter. In this notice she must specify the date of the birth of her child and the date her absence began. The employer may request this notice in writing.

The employee is not required to give notice if she leaves the job for a reason wholly unconnected with her pregnancy after the beginning of the 15th week before the expected week of childbirth. She must, however, give her employer notice of the date on which she actually went into labour if this fell before the 11th week before the expected week of childbirth.

The employee must also provide her employer with a maternity certificate completed by a doctor or registered midwife as evidence of her pregnancy and expected week of childbirth.

Highlight
The employee may also have a contractual right to maternity pay which the employer may set off against SMP.

Remedies for non-payment of SMP

If the employer fails to pay SMP or the employee disputes the amount paid, the employee has the right to require from her employer a written statement of what SMP it considers to be due and reasons why.

If nothing is resolved, the matter may be referred to an adjudication officer. An appeal from the adjudication officeris decision may be made to the Social Security Appeals Tribunal and a further appeal lies on a point of law only to the Social Security Commissioners.

Reclaiming SMP

The employer may reclaim 92% of the gross amount of SMP it has paid by deducting it from the total (i.e. both primary and secondary) Class 1 national insurance contributions due to be paid for all employees in that tax month.

Small employers whose annual gross national insurance bill does not exceed £20,000 are entitled to recover 100% of SMP paid, plus additional compensation of 6.5% of total SMP paid.

Parental leave ▬▬▬▬▬▬▬▬▬

From 15 December 1999, employees will have a right to take 13 weeks unpaid leave for the purposes of caring for a child subject to satisfying certain qualified conditions. At the time of writing the Government has issued draft Regulations, which set out the Government's proposals on Parental Leave and these proposals are set out below. Please note however that these are just proposals and may therefore be subject to change.

What is parental leave?

Parental leave may be taken not just in connection with caring for a child's health. For example, it can be used for the purposes of settling the child into a playgroup, taking a child on holiday or simply staying at home with the child.

Qualifying conditions

A person qualifies for the right to parental leave if they are an employee with at least one year's continuous service and have or expect to have responsibility for a child. A person has responsibility for a child in the following circumstances:

- they are the natural mother or father who were married at the time of birth;

Highlight
If the employer fails to pay SMP or the employee disputes the amount paid, the employee has the right to require from her employer a written statement of what SMP it considers to be due and reasons why.

- they are the natural mother where the parents are not married at time of birth;

- they are the natural father where the parents were not married at the time of birth if the father acquires parental responsibility by court order or agreement with the mother;

- they are a legal guardian;

- they are an adoptive parent.

The relevant child must be born on or after 15th December 1999 or if the child is an adopted child, the child must have been adopted after 15th December 1999. There will no statutory right, even to unpaid leave in respect of children born before 15 December 1999.

It is a fundamental principle that the right to parental leave is an individual one and will be non-transferable. This means that both parents will be able to take up to 13 weeks leave if they are both working, but they will not be able to transfer their leave entitlement so that one employee can take more than 13 weeks and the other less. This is clearly designed to encourage fathers to take parental leave. If a man does not use his leave, it will simply go to waste.

When can parental leave be taken?

Parental leave may be taken before the child's 5th birthday or where they have been adopted for a period of five years or up to the age of 18, whichever is the sooner. The only exception to this is where the employer has postponed parental leave in such circumstances it would be possible to have the postponed leave taken after the 5th birthday or anniversary of adoption cut-off point.

Rights during parental leave

The employment relationship will continue during the leave period although leave may be unpaid. The employment relationship will continue in exactly the same way as in the case of a person taking additional maternity leave, namely, the employee is entitled to the benefit of his or her employer's implied obligation to her of trust and confidence and is also bound by his or her implied obligation of good faith and any express obligation prohibiting disclosure of confidential information or the employee's participation in any competing business.

Right to return to work

The employee has the right to return to his or her old job at the end of the leave period. Alternatively if it is not reasonably practical for him or her to return to his or her old job, he or she has the right to return to another job which is both suitable for the individual and appropriate to do in the circumstances. The terms and conditions on which the individual may return to work after parental leave are as follows:

- on terms and conditions as to remuneration no less favourable than those which would have been applicable to him or her had they not been absent from work;

- with seniority, pension rights and similar rights as they would have been if the period prior to his or her parental leave period were continuous with his or her employment following his or her return to work; and

- otherwise on terms and conditions no less favourable than those which have been applicable to him or her or he or she not been absent from work during the period or parental leave.

Parental leave schemes

The Government has indicated that it would like employers to agree their own parental leave schemes which suit the needs of the business and employees. However, in order to implement a legally enforceable parental scheme it is necessary for this to be entered into by way of a collective agreement or a work force agreement. A collective agreement is one which is reached between the union and an employer as a result of collective bargaining. A workforce agreement is, in effect, a sort of collective agreement which does not involve a union as such. It is an agreement between an employer and his workers which satisfies certain conditions. It has to be in writing and cannot have effect for more than five years. It has to apply to all members of the workforce or all members of the workforce who belong to a particular group. It has to be signed either by representatives of the workforce or group or, where there are 20 or fewer employees, by appropriate representatives or the majority of the employees. This is a fairly complex procedure and it is therefore recommended that if the employer wishes to implement its own parental leave scheme by means of a workforce agreement, further advice should be sought.

If the employer does not implement its own parental leave scheme, the legislation provides that default provisions automatically come into play. These provide that an employee can only exercise his or her entitlement to parental leave if:

- he or she has complied with a reasonable request made the employer to produce evidence of entitlement to take parental leave and age of the child;

- he has given his or her employer proper notice; and

- the employer does not postpone the leave period.

The amount of notice which the employee must give the employer before taking parental leave is:

- at least four weeks before the date on which the period is due to begin where the period of leave is two weeks or less; and

- twice as many weeks before the date on which the period is due to begin as there are weeks in the period where the requested period is going to be longer than two weeks.

However, this does not apply where the leave is to begin on the date on which a child is born or is placed with an employee for adoption. In these specific circumstances, notice must specify the expected week of child birth or placement and the duration of the leave and must be given to the employer at least 13 weeks before the beginning of the expected week of child birth or placement.

Postponement of parental leave

The employer can postpone when a period of parental leave may be taken except where this is to be taken on the birth or placement of a child. In every other circumstance the employer can postpone parental leave if it can show that the business would suffer 'substantial prejudice'. The employer must agree to allow the employee to take the same period of leave within at least six months. The length of notice which the employer must give to the employee to postpone parental leave is a time equal to the amount of leave requested.

Enforcement

An employee has a right to make a claim in the employment tribunal if his employer unreasonably postpones or refuses to attempts to prevent the grant of parental leave. Compensation is such as the tribunal considers just and equitable taking into account the employers behaviour and the loss sustained by the employee as a result of the matter complained of.

Employees also have protection from being subjected to any detriment by any act or omission by the employer because the individual took parental leave. The employee also has protection of automatic unfair dismissal if they are dismissed for a reason relating to the fact that they took parental leave.

There is no statutory requirement for an employer to keep records of when parental leave has been taken. In practice, it is highly likely that organisations will need to keep some sort of record. When an employee changes employers he or she will need to requalify and has no right to take more than 13 weeks for each child in total, including any leave that may have been taken with the previous employer. Therefore it will be sensible when requesting a reference from a previous employer to ask them to provide details of whether parental leave has been taken by the individual, and if so how much.

Time off for dependants

The Employment Relations Act 1999 introduces a right for employees to take a reasonable amount of unpaid leave to deal with incidents involving a dependent. This right is not yet in forced but should be in forced by the end of 1999.

Dependants are defined as the employee's parent, wife, husband or partner, child or someone who lives as part of the family. The employee has the right to time off:

- to help when a dependant is ill or injured;
- to cope when the arrangements for caring for a dependant unexpectedly break down;
- when a dependant gives birth;
- when a dependant dies; or
- to deal with unexpected incident involving a dependent child during school hours, or on a school trip.

In the first two cases, the dependant could also be someone who relies on the employee in the particular emergency.

No predetermined maximum is set on the amount of time off which can be taken. However, it is envisaged by the Government that one or two days will usually be the most that are needed to deal with the immediate issues and sort out longer-term arrangements if necessary.

An employee may complain to an employment tribunal if his or her employer unreasonably refuses to permit him or her to take time off for dependants. If the tribunal find the complaint well founded, compensation may be awarded such as the tribunal considers just and equitable in all these circumstances having regard to the employers default and any loss sustained by the employee which is attributable to the matters complained of.

Sickness benefit

Subject to satisfying certain conditions, all employees are entitled to receive statutory sick pay (SSP) from their employers when they are absent from work for four or more consecutive days up to a limit of 28 weeks in a three-year period. Unless the employee has a contractual right to normal pay, SSP is all the employer is obliged to pay him or her during sickness. The model contract included in this Guide (see Appendix 10) provides for normal remuneration for a limited period. The current weekly rate of SSP is £59.55 is verifiable by contacting the Department of Education or ACAS (see Appendix 30)

Eligibility

Highlight

Employees aged under 16 or over 65 are not eligible to receive statutory sick pay.

Employees are not eligible for statutory sick pay if:

- they are aged under 16 or over 65;

- they have a contract of services which is for a specified period of three months or less;

- their average weekly pay is below the point at which national insurance contributions are payable (currently £62 per week);

- they have received social security benefit in the 57 days before the first day of sickness;

- they have not yet commenced working;

- they become sick while pregnant during the statutory maternity pay period (see chapter 3);

- they have been due SSP for 28 weeks from a former employee and the last day on which SSP was paid is eight weeks ago or less;

- they become sick during a trade dispute at their workplace, unless they can prove they have no direct interest in the dispute;

- they are in legal custody.

If notified that an ineligible employee has been absent for four or more consecutive days an employer must send a form to the employee within seven days of being notified which explains why SSP is not payable. The employee may then claim incapacity benefit.

Requirements for qualification

SSP is only payable:

- if the employee has been incapable of work for four or more consecutive days (this is known as a period of incapacity for work or 'PIW');

- if the employee has notified the employer of his absence and given evidence of his incapacity i.e. doctor's note (in accordance with any rules laid down by the employer which must be made available to all employees);

- for days on which the employee would normally be required to work;

- during a 'period of entitlement', i.e. a period commencing with the start of PIW and ending:

    (i)   when the employee returns to work;

    (ii) when the maximum entitlement of 28 weeks SSP has been paid (if the employee is still sick in these circumstances, he or she shall become entitled to incapacity benefit);

    (iii) with the expiry or termination of the employee's contract of employment;

    (iv) when the employee becomes entitled to maternity allowance or statutory maternity pay (see chapter 3); or

    (v)   if the employee goes into legal custody.

If there is a good cause for delay, the employee has one calender month to notify the employer of sickness absence (this may be extended to 91 days if it is not reasonably practicable to notify the employer within one month).

If there are less than eight weeks between any periods of incapacity for work, they are linked and count as one PIW for SSP purposes.

Highlight
If there is a good cause for delay, the employee has one calender month to notify the employer of sickness absence.

When calculating whether the maximum entitlement has been paid, periods of entitlement to SSP from a previous employer are taken into account:

- where less than eight weeks have elapsed between the last day the previous employer was liable to pay the employee SSP and the start of the PIW with the new employer; and

- the employee has provided the new employer with a leaver's statement (Form *SSP1(L)*) or the employer has issued such a statement to the employee.

Employers must issue a form *SSP(I)(T)* to employees whose maximum entitlement to 28 weeks is about to expire, no later than the 23rd week of sickness.

SSP attracts income tax and national insurance contributions.

Employers cannot require employees to contract out of their rights to SSP or contribute towards SSP payments. Failure to comply with the obligation to pay SSP can amount to a criminal offence.

Employers' right to reimbursement of statutory sickness payments

All employers may reclaim the amount paid out as SSP to the extent that it exceeds 13% of their liability to pay national insurance contributions (both employees and employers) for the month in question.

Records

Highlight
All employers must keep records of the dates on which their employees are absent due to sickness.

All employers must keep records of the dates on which their employees are absent due to sickness for three years. The penalty for failure to meet these obligations is a fine of up to £1000 plus £40 per day for as long as the offence continues. Employers who produce false information concerning SSP face a fine of up to £5,000 or a maximum of 3 months in prison.

Employers have freedom from operating the SSP scheme if they pay sick employees contractual remuneration at or above the prescribed rate of SSP.

Discrimination

The law on discrimination has an enormous effect in employment. The UK's membership in the European Union (EU) means that a high level of protection from discrimination exists for employees. An employee who complains of discrimination in whatever way can pursue legal action in an employment tribunal and no qualifying period is necessary in order to bring such a claim. Discrimination claims are not subject to any maximum award and are therefore increasing in number and value.

UK legislation that governs discrimination complies with the EU law; when new EU laws are introduced UK laws must be amended accordingly.

There is currently protection from discrimination in relation to sex, gender reassignment (i.e. 'sex change'), marital status, race, disability and trade union membership.

There is currently no law against treating employees or prospective employees less favourably because of their age, although a voluntary Code of Practice has recently been published to tackle the problem of age discrimination. In addition, restrictions on age can in some circumstances amount to indirect sex discrimination (see below).

Although there has been much pressure in the UK for a law to protect homosexuals being discriminated against on the grounds of their sexual preference, nothing has yet been enacted. EU law as it currently stands, offers no protection and no remedy. However, proposals are being made for legislation to be introduced to deal with discrimination on the grounds of sexual orientation.

The areas of discrimination that are considered in this chapter are:

- Sex discrimination and discrimination on the grounds of marriage
- Race discrimination
- Equal pay
- Disability discrimination
- Harassment

Sex discrimination and discrimination on the grounds of marriage

Discrimination on the grounds of sex or marriage is made unlawful by the Sex Discrimination Act 1975 (SDA) which forbids it at every stage of employment (i.e. advertising vacancies, engagement of employees, promotion, training and other opportunities, and dismissal). Employment has a wider definition in the SDA than other employment protection legislation, protecting not only individuals who are employees but also individuals working under a contract for services and partners in a partnership. In addition, other organisations, including trade unions, trade or professional associations and employment agencies must also observe the provisions of the SDA.

Individuals who are not protected by the SDA in their employment are:

- persons who work wholly or mainly outside Great Britain;

- police officers in relation to height requirements and uniform or uniform allowances;

- prison officers in relation to height requirements;

- ministers of religion if employment is limited to one sex in order to comply with the doctrines of the religion or to avoid offending the religious sensibilities of a significant number of its followers.

Definition of discrimination

There are three recognised forms of discrimination:

    (a) direct discrimination

    (b) indirect discrimination

    (c) victimisation

In deciding whether discrimination has occurred, the position of the person allegedly discriminated against is compared to that of a person of similar skill and qualification. The intention or motive of the alleged discriminator is irrelevant. The SDA protects males as well as females.

(a) Direct discrimination

Direct discrimination is easy to recognise: it occurs where an employee has received less favourable treatment and would not have but for his or her sex or marital status. For there to be direct discrimination, the person's sex or marital status is the basis of the particular decision which results in the individual being deprived in some way and which gives

Highlight
Discrimination on the grounds of sex or marriage is made unlawful by the SDA which forbids such discrimination at every stage of employment.

Highlight
To decide whether discrimination has taken place, the position of the person allegedly discriminated against will be compared with that of a person of similar skill and qualification.

rise to less favourable treatment. It is the treatment itself rather than its consequences which must be different and less favourable.

An individual may exercise unconscious prejudices, because of his or her upbringing and perceptions, without being aware of the fact and this can amount to direct discrimination. It is important that employers give training in order to avoid such prejudices.

The burden of proof for direct discrimination involves the individual complaining of discrimination having to establish the case and then the employer giving an explanation which attempts to justify the alleged discriminatory act. If no explanation is forthcoming, or an unsatisfactory explanation is provided, then the employment tribunal is entitled to infer that the discrimination did in fact take place.

Dress requirements. The test of whether or not the individual would have received the same treatment, but for his or her sex, has proved problematic where the treatment complained of is the imposition of dress requirement. Therefore, there is no discrimination where male and female employees are subject to different but comparable dress requirements.

Maternity cases. Unfavourable treatment on the grounds of an employee's pregnancy or for other maternity-related reasons is direct discrimination contrary to the SDA. There is no need for a comparison with a male employee: once a female employee has established that her treatment amounted to direct discrimination, no question of justification for this treatment can arise.

This occurs when a woman is engaged by the employer for an indefinite period. However, if a woman is employed for a single fixed-term period or to fulfil a particular task, it is uncertain whether the employer would be guilty of discrimination if: the woman was denied employment during which time she would be unavailable for work because of her pregnancy or, if after engaging the woman for such a period, the employer discovered that she was pregnant and subsequently cancelled the agreement.

(b) Indirect discrimination

Indirect discrimination covers other forms of less obvious discriminatory treatment. Indirect discrimination takes place where:

- an employer imposes a condition or requirement with which the individual cannot comply and which is to his or her detriment;

- the condition or requirement can be shown to have a disproportionate impact in excluding others of the individual's sex or marital status; and

- the condition cannot be justified irrespective of the individual's sex or marital status.

Highlight
Indirect discrimination takes place where an employer imposes a condition or requirement with which the individual cannot comply.

For example, indirect sex discrimination would take place where an employer imposed a requirement for all employees to be subject to a five foot maximum height requirement. A much larger proportion of women than men would be able to meet this requirement and the employer would have to justify the reason for imposing such a condition. If the reason was because the job was to crew a boat with very low ceilings such a requirement would probably be justified. But, if the reason was because the employer only wished to provide one size of uniform, the employer would be indirectly discriminating against men.

Justification requires an objective balance between the discriminatory effect of the condition or requirement and the reasonable needs of the employer who is applying it. Justification is a 'matter of fact' for the employment tribunal, which means that one tribunal might reach one conclusion and another might reach a different conclusion.

Age. Although there is no law against age discrimination, placing restrictions on age can, in some circumstances, amount to indirect sex discrimination. This has been the case where an employer required a maximum age limit of 28 for a job. An employment appeal tribunal held this was indirectly discriminatory because in practice it was harder for women to comply with it than men, since women in their 20s are commonly fully occupied with child-bearing.

(c) Victimisation

An employer would be guilty of sex discrimination by victimisation if it treated any employee less favourably than others because that employee had brought, or threatened to bring proceedings, give evidence or information, or take any action or make any allegation concerning the employer, with reference to the SDA or the Equal Pay Act 1970 (EPA).

Exceptions to sex discrimination protection

The law recognises that there are some circumstances where there may be a good reason to give favourable treatment to a particular sex. In particular, there are two areas:

- *Positive discrimination*. If an employer identifies that one sex is not properly represented within certain work areas, it may try to encourage individuals of that particular sex to apply, by providing training or through an advertising campaign. Before doing this, the employer must be able to show that in the previous 12 months there have been either no individuals of that particular sex, or only a small proportion of them, carrying out the work in question. If not, the positive action will be discriminatory.

• *Genuine occupational qualifications.* For some jobs being of a certain sex is a requirement, as set out in chapter 1. But attitudes and cultures are changing and an exception which was once acceptable may no longer be so. The applicability of the genuine occupational qualification exception should be considered every time a vacancy is advertised.

Employer responsibility for discrimination

Under the SDA an employer is liable for anything done by his employees in the course of their employment, whether or not it was done with the employer's knowledge or approval. This ensures that the employer takes responsibility for preventing discrimination at work (in the SDA 'employment' has a wide definition and includes any contract personally to execute work and is not confined to a contract of service). However, it is a defence if the employer can prove that he took such steps as were practicable to prevent an employee from doing a certain act.

If the employer wishes to rely on this defence, it must be shown that positive steps have been taken to address the possibility of discrimination occurring in the work place. For example, the employer should introduce and adhere to an equal opportunities policy which incorporates a sexual and racial harassment policy (see Appendix 17). All employees should be aware of such policies and be given training in their obligations not to discriminate. Disciplinary action should be taken against those who do discriminate.

The individual discriminator still risks that action will be taken against him or her whether or not the employer is found responsible. An individual who wishes to pursue an action for discrimination may issue proceedings in an employment tribunal against his or her employer and against the individual discriminator. However, if the individual discriminator can prove that the action taken was based on an assurance from the employer that it was not discriminatory, he or she will not be held liable for discrimination.

Other unlawful acts under the SDA

It is unlawful to do any of the following:

• to knowingly aid and abet someone in unlawful discrimination; the person who committed the discriminatory act has the defence that he or she acted reasonably, relying on a statement by the other that the act would not be unlawful;

• to instruct someone to discriminate over whom one has authority or to someone who normally acts in accordance with one's wishes;

- to induce or attempt to induce someone to discriminate; such inducements may include offering either benefits or detriments.

No contracting-out

Employers are not allowed to exclude or limit any provision of the SDA in a contract of employment. If they do it would have no effect, leaving the employee at liberty to bring a complaint under the SDA against the employer in an employment tribunal.

Gender Re-Assignment

The SDA also prohibits discrimination on the grounds of gender re-assignment. This applies to people intending to undergo, undergoing or having undergone a sex change. There is no protection from indirect discrimination on these grounds, and genuine occupational qualifications apply.

The Equal Opportunities Commission (EOC)

The SDA establishes the EOC, which has the following duties:

- to work towards the elimination of discrimination;

- to promote equality of opportunity between men and women generally; and

- to keep under review the work of the SDA and the EPA (for more details on the EPA see page 68).

Codes of Practice. The EOC has issued a code of practice and guidance notes for the elimination of sex and marriage discrimination and the promotion of equality of opportunity in employment. Employers are advised to review the code and guidance notes and to put into place its recommendations. A breach of the recommendations does not of itself render a person liable to proceedings, but it may be taken into account by an employment tribunal when determining whether or not discrimination has occurred.

Investigations. As part of its general duties, the EOC may if it thinks fit, and if required by the Secretary of State for Education and Employment, conduct a formal investigation, (which may be in relation to a particular organisation), where it considers there has been a breach of the provisions of the SDA or the EPA.

Non-discrimination notice. The EOC can issue a non-discrimination notice if it finds that a person has committed or is committing an unlawful discriminatory act or practice, a breach of the provisions relating to advertising, or of a term modified (or included) by virtue of an equality clause or has given instructions to discriminate or pressure to discriminate. This notice may require a person to stop committing

Highlight
Employers are not allowed to exclude or limit any provision of the SDA in a contract of employment.

any such acts, or to change any of his or her practices or arrangements, to inform the EOC that he or she has effected those changes and what they are, and to take such steps to inform people affected by those practices or arrangements. The EOC cannot issue a non-discrimination notice without (i) informing the relevant person of its intention and the grounds of the notice, (ii) allowing the relevant person at least 28 days in which to make representations and (iii) taking into account all the representations made by him.

Employers are advised to ensure that they do not breach any of the provisions of the SDA or the EPA. If they do, and are informed of a proposal to issue a notice, they must take action to prevent the discrimination. If a notice has been issued and the employers do not wish to challenge it, they should comply with it as soon as possible. An employer has a right of appeal against any requirement of a non-discrimination notice.

A register of non-discrimination notices which have been issued is available for inspection and for copying from the Equal Opportunities Commission, listed in Appendix 30.

Race discrimination

Discrimination on racial grounds is made unlawful by the Race Relations Act 1976 (RRA) which reflects many of the principles and rules contained in the SDA examined in the first section of this chapter. The RRA forbids less favourable treatment of individuals on racial grounds at every stage of employment. Like the SDA, the RRA protects not only individual employees but also individuals working under a contract for services and partners in a partnership (where the partnership consists of six or more partners). In addition, trade unions, trade or professional associations, employment agencies and other organisations must also observe the provisions of the RRA.

Highlight
The RRA forbids less favourable treatment of individuals on racial grounds at every stage of employment.

Individuals not protected by the RRA are:

- those who work wholly or mainly outside Great Britain;

- individuals employed by a private household (with the exception of discrimination by victimisation, see page 62).

Definition of discrimination

The three forms of discrimination in relation to sex and on the grounds of marriage apply equally to race. Whereas the definitions of sex and marriage are straightforward, what is meant by racial grounds requires further explanation. If a decision is based on an individual's colour, race, nationality or national origins, or ethnic origins it is a decision based on racial grounds and could be discriminatory.

The meaning of 'ethnic origins' needs clarifying. It has been held that a group has an ethnic origin if it has certain characteristics:

- a long shared history; and

- a cultural tradition.

Additional relevant characteristics are:

- a common geographical origin or descent from a small number of common ancestors;

- a common language not necessarily peculiar to the group;

- a common literature peculiar to the group;

- a common religion different from that of the neighbouring or surrounding community;

- being a minority or being in an oppressed or dominant group in a large community.

It has been held in the courts that Sikhs are an ethnic group, as are Jews and Gypsies, but at present Rastafarians have been held not to fall within what can be considered an ethnic group.

In a sex discrimination claim a comparison is made between a female employee and a male employee in equivalent circumstances to decide whether the treatment of one is less favourable. In a race discrimination claim, the comparison must be between the person of the racial or ethnic group and a job applicant or employee who is not of that ethnic or racial group, but whose circumstances are the same, similar or not materially different.

(a) Direct discrimination

The principle of direct discrimination as already examined in relation to sex and marriage discrimination, applies here: in a race discrimination claim the less favourable treatment is obviously on racial grounds and the test is whether, but for the individual's racial origin, ethnic origin, nationality, national origin or colour, he or she would not have been subject to that treatment.

(b) Indirect discrimination

Again, the principle of indirect discrimination as examined in relation to sex and marriage discrimination applies to race discrimination. Indirect discrimination will occur if a condition or requirement is imposed which has a disproportionate impact on a particular racial group so that a considerably smaller proportion of members of that group can comply

Highlight
In a race discrimination claim, the comparison must be between the person of the racial or ethnic group and a job applicant or employee who is not of that ethnic or racial group, but whose circumstances are the same, similar or not materially different.

than those outside it, and it cannot be objectively justified on some basis other than colour, race, nationality or ethnic or national origins.

Whether someone can comply with a condition or requirement is decided by what he or she can do in practice rather than in theory.

The question of whether indirect discrimination is objectively justifiable is (as with sex and marriage discrimination) one of fact for an employment tribunal. The employment tribunal must strike a balance between the discriminatory effect of the condition or requirement being imposed and the reasonable needs of the employer applying it.

(c) Victimisation

An employer would be guilty of race discrimination by victimisation if he or she treated any employee less favourably than others because that employee has already or threatens to bring proceedings, give evidence or information, take any action or make any allegation concerning the employer with reference to the RRA.

Exceptions to race discrimination protection

As with sex discrimination, the law recognises that in some circumstances there may be a good reason to give favourable treatment to a particular race. There are two areas where exceptions to the law against race discrimination exist:

- *Positive discrimination.* If an employer identifies a particular racial group as not being properly represented within certain work areas, he may try to encourage individuals of that group to apply by providing training or through an advertising campaign. The employer must be able to show that in the previous 12 months there have been either no individuals of the racial group or only a small proportion of them carrying out the particular work in question. If this exception does not apply then the positive action will be discriminatory. A booklet entitled *What is Positive Action?* published by the Race Relations Employment Advisory Service provides further explanation of positive race discrimination.

- *Genuine occupational qualifications.* For some jobs belonging to a certain racial group is a requirement, as set out in chapter 1. The number of jobs where a person's race is a genuine occupational qualification is not as high as that concerning a person's sex. The warning that attitudes and cultures are changing should also be remembered in relation to race. The applicability of the genuine occupational qualification exception should be considered every time a vacancy is advertised.

Employer responsibility for discrimination

The same principle applies under the RRA as previously described in relation to the SDA in the first section of this chapter. For an employer relying on this defence, regard will be given to whether a written policy on race discrimination has been issued to employees, whether training has been given and whether disciplinary action has been taken against those guilty of race discrimination.

Other unlawful acts under the RRA

The unlawful acts listed on page 63 in relation to the SDA equally apply to the RRA.

No contracting-out

The ban on contractual clauses excluding or limiting provisions of the SDA equally applies to excluding or limiting those of the RRA.

The Commission for Racial Equality (CRE)

The RRA establishes the CRE, which has the following duties:

- to work towards the elimination of discrimination;
- to promote equality of opportunity between persons of different racial groups;
- to keep under review the working of the RRA.

These duties are the same as the duties of the EOC in relation to sex discrimination and the points previously made about codes of practice, investigations and non-discrimination notices apply equally to the CRE. The address of the CRE is listed in Appendix 30.

Equal pay ━━━━━━━━━━━━━━━━━━━━━━

The Equal Pay Act 1970 (EPA) provides that discrimination between the sexes in the terms of their contracts of employment is unlawful. This typically occurs in matters such as salary, bonus payments and benefits.

The EPA has been criticised because its provisions are too complex and it takes many years for claims under the Act to reach a conclusion.

The EPA protects males as well as females and it benefits employees under a contract of employment as well as self-employed people under a contract for services. It does not apply to individuals who work wholly or mainly outside Great Britain nor does it apply to members of the armed forces.

Highlight
The EPA protects males as well as females and it benefits employees under a contract of employment as well as self-employed people under a contract for services.

The EOC has recently published a Code of Practice on Pay which aims to provide practical guidance on good practice in relation to equal pay, which includes a suggested equal pay policy.

Meaning of equality

An individual can claim equality if he or she can establish one of the following:

- that he or she is carrying out work which is the same or broadly similar to work being carried out by someone of the opposite sex in the same employment; or

- that he or she is carrying out work which has been rated as equal, through a job evaluation study, to work being carried out by someone of the opposite sex in the same employment; or

- that he or she is carrying out work which is of equal value to the work of someone of the opposite sex in the same employment.

Comparison. The comparison must be with a person of the opposite sex who exists (or has existed) who is doing like work, work graded as equal or work of equal value and who is employed by the same employer (or an associated employer) either at the same establishment or at an establishment within Great Britain where, in general, common terms and conditions are observed.

Defence. An employer can successfully defend a claim under the EPA if it can:

- prove that the work is not like or similar, not rated as equal or not of equal value; or

- prove that the difference between the complainant's contract and the comparison contract is genuinely due to a material factor which is not the difference in sex; this requires that the employer show the reason for the factor and that the factor identified objectively justifies the difference in the contracts.

Equality clause. If an individual can establish that one of the above three justifications for equality applies and his or her contract contains terms less beneficial than those enjoyed by the comparator of the opposite sex, or which omits a beneficial term enjoyed by the comparator, he or she can apply to an industrial tribunal to have an equality clause implied into his or her contract. Such a clause modifies the individual's contract so that it is equivalent to the comparator's contract.

Other remedies. In addition to an equality clause in the contract, a person successful in a complaint under the EPA may be awarded compensation for loss suffered in the past as a result of lack of equality. There is a limit of two years' back pay for compensation awarded under the EPA (plus interest for half the period from when the complainant first suffered loss as a result of contravention of the EPA and the date of the complaint). However, recent case law has held that the limit of two years' back pay is incompatible with European law, and has awarded back pay for a period of six years.

Disability discrimination

The Disability Discrimination Act 1996 (DDA) protects people with disabilities against discrimination in all aspects of employment. Breach of the DDA can result in a complaint to an employment tribunal, regardless of length of service and with no limit to the amount of compensation. The Government has produced information booklets on different sections of the DDA; these and the code of practice are available by calling 0345 622633.

Highlight
Breach of the DDA can result in a complaint to an employment tribunal with no limit to the amount of compensation.

The main consequence of the DDA in relation to employment is that it is now unlawful for an employer of 15 or more employees to discriminate against a disabled person – or someone who has been disabled in the past – in recruitment, terms and conditions of employment, promotion, training (or other benefits), dismissal or by subjecting him or her to any disadvantage. It is important that the term 'employees' be widely interpreted to included the self-employed and those engaged under a contract of service or apprenticeship (as it is with other discrimination legislation). The provisions of the DDA do not apply to employers of fewer than 15 people and there are some categories of employees to whom they do not apply.

Code of practice

This gives practical guidance to employers on fulfilling their new obligations and avoiding possible claims of discrimination. Breaches of the code are admissible as evidence in employment tribunal hearings.

What kind of discrimination is covered by the DDA?

A disability is defined in this context as a physical or mental impairment which has a substantial and long-term adverse effect on a person's ability to carry out normal day-to-day activities. Such a broad definition includes learning disabilities, mental illnesses (if recognised by a respected body of medical opinion), impairments which come and go if the actual effect is likely to recur (e.g. rheumatoid arthritis) and severe disfigurements. People with progressive conditions are covered from the moment the condition leads to impairment of their ability to carry out day-to-day activities. The definition specifically excludes some impairments, such as alcohol or drug addiction, hayfever and self-disfigurement (i.e. tattoos).

What is discrimination in this context?

An employer discriminates against a disabled person if:

- it treats him or her less favourably, for a reason related to the person's present or past disability, than it treats or would treat a person to whom that reason does not apply and the employer cannot show that this treatment is justified;

- it fails to comply with a new duty of making reasonable adjustments in relation to disabled persons, and the employer cannot show that this failure is justified.

Justification

Less favourable treatment of a disabled person is justified if the reason for it is both 'material' to the circumstances of the case and 'substantial'. According to the code this means that the reason has to relate to the individual circumstances in question and must not be trivial or minor. The code gives some examples, including these:

Someone who is blind is not shortlisted for a job involving computers because the employer thinks blind people cannot use them. The employer makes no effort to consider the individual circumstances. This general assumption that blind people cannot use computers would not in itself be a material (i.e. justified) reason because it is not related to the particular circumstances of the applicant.

Someone who has psoriasis (a skin condition) is rejected for a job involving modelling cosmetics on a part of the body which, in his case, is severely disfigured by the condition. This would be justified if his appearance were incompatible with the purpose of the work. The reason is material to the individual circumstances of the case and it is substantial.

Employers may offer a disabled person less favourable terms of employment if there is a material and substantial reason for doing so and no reasonable adjustments can be made to remove that reason. For example, if, despite any reasonable adjustments, a disabled employee has a significantly lower output than other employees the employer can pay that employee less than the others.

Reasonable adjustments

If any physical feature of the employer's premises or other arrangements causes a substantial disadvantage to a disabled person the employer must make reasonable adjustments to prevent it. 'Arrangements' includes all that an employer arranges in recruiting employees and in the workplace, for example selection and interview procedures and working conditions.

Appropriate adjustments might include altering premises, re-allocating duties, transferring staff to fill an existing vacancy, altering working hours, assigning someone to a different place of work, allowing absences from office training, acquiring or modifying equipment, modifying instructions or manuals, modifying procedures for testing or assessment and providing a reader or supervision. Whether it is reasonable for an employer to have to make a particular adjustment will depend upon a number of factors:

- how effective it would be in preventing the disadvantage

- how practical it is

- the financial and other costs and the disruption likely to be caused

- the extent of the financial resources of the employer

- the availability of assistance to make adjustment

National Disability Council

This advises the Government on relevant issues, including the operation of legislation, although it does not have as many powers as the Equal Opportunities Commission or Commission for Racial Equality in investigating or supporting individual's complaints.

Harassment ——————————————————

Racial and sexual harassment have been held to be unlawful direct discrimination by the RRA and the SDA even though neither are defined as distinct offences under those Acts.

There is an increased awareness of the issues involved in racial and sexual harassment and recent years have shown a significant rise in complaints to employment tribunals. If the complaint is serious, employment tribunals will award high damages. Therefore, it is crucial for employers to take steps to prevent harassment occurring in their work place. Where it does occur they should deal with it appropriately.

Highlight

If any physical feature of the employer's premises or other arrangements causes a substantial disadvantage to a disabled person - compared to a non-disabled person - the employer must make reasonable adjustments to prevent it.

Definition

Although there is no legal definition of racial and sexual harassment it is accepted that behaviour that falls within the scope is quite varied, including physical, verbal and non-verbal conduct. The conduct must be unwanted by the recipient and used, to the recipient's detriment, as a basis for employment decisions.

More detailed guidance can be found in the European Commission's recommendation and code of practice *Protection of the Dignity of Men and Women at Work* in relation to sexual harassment and the CRE's *Racial Harassment At Work* in relation to racial harassment.

Employer responsibility for harassment

Racial and sexual harassment fall under discrimination legislation and therefore the employer is liable for the acts of its employees in the course of their employment. It is not always clear whether an act of harassment should be regarded as 'in the course of employment'. If the harasser is acting in a supervisory role, his or her act of harassment is more likely to be deemed to be in the course of employment than if the harasser is in a subordinate position.

Employers, however, can avoid liability for the action of an employee in the course of employment if they can prove that they took such steps as were reasonably practicable to prevent the employee from committing a certain act, or from committing acts of that description in the course of his or her employment. This defence has been examined earlier in this chapter.

Preventing harassment

Highlight
Employers should have an equal opportunities policy and a sexual and racial harassment policy which defines harassment and states that it should not occur.

The best way to avoid racial and sexual harassment complaints is to ensure that harassment does not occur in the first place. Employers should have an equal opportunities policy and a sexual and racial harassment policy which define harassment and state that it should not occur (see Appendix 17). Employees must be made aware of the existence of these policies, educated about harassment and warned of its consequences.

Employees should be aware that acts of harassment are taken very seriously by the employer and will be considered gross misconduct.

Dealing with harassment complaints

Complaints of harassment can be very disruptive to the work place and must be dealt with very carefully. If an employee complains of harassment, consider whether an informal approach to the harasser would be appropriate, i.e. if it is a less serious complaint or the first instance of harassment. Consider whether the person complaining of harassment wants an informal approach or would rather more formal action be taken.

If an informal warning is appropriate, the alleged harasser should be consulted to explain that the conduct is upsetting the employee, and that it is considered harassment and must not continue. He or she should also be warned that the matter will be kept under review. He or she must be shown the policy which is in place and warned that if matters do not improve disciplinary action will be taken. The person who has complained of harassment should be kept informed of the warning given and told to inform the employer if he or she has any further complaints against the alleged harasser.

Where an informal approach is inappropriate or if the complainant wants formal action taken, the disciplinary procedure should be followed in the following way:

- Ask the complainant for a full statement.

- Suspend the alleged harasser pending the investigation of the complaint (if appropriate).

- Take statements from all staff who can provide evidence about the alleged harassment.

- Interview the alleged harasser and invite him or her to provide a statement. A disciplinary hearing to give the alleged harasser the opportunity to answer the complaint or justify or excuse his or her conduct will be necessary if there is substance to or doubt in relation to the matters complained of.

- Very often there will be no witnesses and it will be one word against the other, leaving it to the employer to decide which version to believe.

- If the conclusion is that harassment has taken place consider a penalty. In serious cases the likely outcome will be dismissal although, in some circumstances, it may be appropriate to transfer the harasser. With harassment of a less serious nature, a final written warning will be appropriate.

Highlight
If an employee complains of harassment, consider whether an informal approach to the harasser would be appropriate ie in the case of a less serious complaint or the first instance of harassment.

Criminal Justice & Public Order Act 1994

Under this Act, there is now a criminal offence of intentional harassment, alarm or distress which renders racial, sexual and all other forms of harassment including harassment against homosexuals and disabled persons at work and in the street a criminal offence punishable by six months' imprisonment or a fine of £5,000. It is necessary to prove that the harasser's action was intentional and also that someone was actually harassed.

This offence relates to harassment by an individual and is of little use in the employment context, although employers may be under a duty to inform employees of their rights under the Act.

Protection from Harassment Act 1997

Under this Act, is is now an offence for someone to pursue a course of conduct which amounts to harassment of another and which he or she knows, or ought to know, amounts to harassment. In addition to providing for harassers to be subject potentially to a fine of up to six months' imprisonment, the Act creates a number of civil remedies including damages and restraining order backed by powers of arrest.

Termination of employment

All employers must at some time deal with the termination of contracts of employment. Many employers associate termination of employment with the anxiety and expense of proceedings being brought against them by a disgruntled employee. This does not have to be the case if the employer is aware of the contractual and statutory duties in relation to termination so that termination can be effected in a legally acceptable way.

This chapter describes the various ways contracts of employment can be brought to an end, the potential problems that can arise and the recommended procedure for avoiding such problems. The chapter is divided into sections as follows:

- Dismissal

- Other forms of termination

- Claims and settlements for termination

Dismissal

In the context of termination of employment, 'dismissal' is defined as occurring in the following situations, each of which is discussed in subsequent sections:

(a) the employee's contract of employment is terminated by the employer with or without notice;

(b) the employee works under a fixed-term contract and the term expires without renewal under the same contract;

(c) the employee terminates his or her own contract, with or without notice, in circumstances such that he or she is entitled to by reason of the employer's conduct. This is known as 'constructive dismissal' (see page 80).

'Unfair dismissal' arises from statutory rights (see page 84 for details) whereas 'wrongful dismissal' arises from contractual rights (see page 88 for details).

(a) Termination by employer with or without notice

Termination with notice

The proper notice to be given is often specified in the contract of employment; the written statement given to the employee must include the length of notice which the employee is obliged to give and entitled to receive (see page 26). However, if a notice period has not been expressly agreed, there is an implied term that it may be terminated upon reasonable notice. Just what is reasonable notice will depend on the case in question, taking into account the seniority, age, length of service, remuneration of the employee and what is usual in the industry.

Whatever the contractual provisions for termination of the contract, the notice actually given must not be less than the statutory minimum period of notice (see page 26). If proper notice is given there can be no claim for wrongful dismissal. However, there may still be a valid claim for unfair dismissal if proper notice is given. Conversely, a dismissal may be fair even though proper notice is not given.

Pay in lieu of notice

It is common for an employer terminating an employment contract to want the employee to cease working immediately. This is because very often an employee who knows he or she is leaving will not carry out his or her work effectively and can be disruptive in the work place. In these circumstances it is usual for the employer to pay the employee a sum in lieu of notice or compensation for failure to give notice.

Sometimes the contract will provide that it may be terminated either by notice, or without notice on payment of a sum in lieu. In these circumstances the employee is entitled to the pay in lieu under a contractual obligation on the employer to make the payment, and tax and National Insurance deductions should be made in the usual way.

Usually however, there is nothing in a contract relating to making payments in lieu. In these circumstances payment may be considered as compensation for the employer's breach of contract in not giving notice and in some circumstances may be paid tax-free up to a limit of £30,000. It is not always entirely clear whether payment should be seen as compensation or as payment in lieu of notice so it is worth seeking advice on this point.

Highlight
Whatever the contractual provisions for termination of the contract, the notice actually given must not be less than the statutory minimum period of notice.

When compensation is being paid free of tax, the fact that it is compensation should be stated to the employee in writing, with a condition that the employee agrees to reimburse the employer in the event that it becomes liable to pay tax in relation to the payment. See the example letter at Appendix 27 from an employer dismissing with payment in lieu of notice. If there is any doubt about whether or not the sum should be paid tax-free, clearance can be sought from the Inland Revenue in advance.

Compensation must be assessed to put the employee in the same position, with respect to damages for the employer's breach of contract of employment, as if the contract had been performed during the notice period. Therefore, it is not only the employee's salary but also all benefits, such as company car, that must be included in the calculation.

Termination without notice

Highlight
Dismissal without notice is a breach of contract by the employer rendering him or her liable in damages for wrongful dismissal.

Dismissal without notice is a breach of contract by the employer rendering him or her liable in damages for wrongful dismissal (see page 88). The exception is when the employee has acted in gross misconduct in which case the employer is justified in dismissing with immediate effect. A contract often expresses the right of the employer to dismiss the employee without notice; but in any event the employer should give its employees a clear indication of what type of conduct it regards as gross misconduct. This will depend upon the type of employment in question, as conduct which constitutes gross misconduct in one area of employment might not be considered to be so serious in another. Examples may be included in the disciplinary procedure, although it should be made clear that the examples given are not exhaustive. Examples of gross misconduct are: theft, damage to the employer's property, incapacity for work due to being under the influence of alcohol or illegal drugs, physical assault and gross insubordination.

(b) Expiry of a fixed-term contract

A fixed-term contract will automatically terminate at the end of the term, without any notice having to be given. However, if a fixed-term contract is not renewed the employee may have a valid claim for redundancy pay or in respect of unfair dismissal. The exception to this is if the employee has agreed to exclude his or her unfair dismissal rights and/or statutory redundancy payment rights (see page 32). Please note however that any exclusion of unfair dismissal rights in fixed term contracts will shortly be invalid under new legislation.

A fixed-term contract can be extended where an employee remains in the employment after the expiry of the term. In these circumstances, contract of employment will continue with an implied term that it may be terminated by either party giving reasonable notice.

(c) Constructive dismissal

If the employer's conduct is such that it is in fundamental breach of the contract of employment, the employee may resign with immediate effect. In such circumstances the employee may have a valid claim for unfair dismissal and for wrongful dismissal.

Resigned or constructively dismissed?

Where an employee complains of unfair and constructive dismissal, it is common for the employer to argue that the employee resigned and dismissal did not occur. The employee would have to prove that the employer's conduct clearly breached and repudiated the contract entitling him or her to leave without notice (whether he or she gave notice or not).

The employee must have considered that the contract was at an end because of the employer's conduct. The employer's conduct is sufficient to justify the employee leaving and complaining of constructive dismissal if it:

- was a significant breach going to the root of the contract of employment; or

- showed that the employer no longer intended to be bound by one or more of the essential terms of the contract.

Very often constructive dismissal occurs as a result of a breach of the implied terms of trust and confidence in the contract (i.e. a breakdown in the employment relationship). This can be caused by a single action by the employer (such as verbal abuse) or by a series of less serious actions which together amount to a breach of the terms.

If an employer makes a statement of clear intention to breach an essential term of the contract, the employee can leave and claim constructive dismissal based on an anticipatory breach of the contract.

The employee must leave quickly because of the breach of contract. If he or she does not leave soon after the incident or incidents complained of the employer can argue that the employee accepted the alleged breach and therefore, no constructive dismissal will have occurred.

Other terminations

(a) Resignation

Resignation by an employee should be with notice. The period of notice to be given by an employee is subject to a statutory minimum of one week, although the contractual notice period will in many cases be longer. The contractual notice period may be either expressly agreed upon or implied. If implied, the notice period must be considered a reasonable period under all the circumstances.

An employee is entitled to continue to receive all benefits for the notice period provided he or she is ready and willing to work for that period. However, the parties may agree that the employee may stop working before the end of the full notice period.

An employer is advised to ensure that clear words of resignation are used. Words spoken in the heat of the moment should not be relied upon as terminating the employment, as they may not amount to a resignation. The employment would then be deemed to be terminated by dismissal by the employer and the employee would have a right to make a claim of unfair dismissal.

The employer should accept resignation and communicate this acceptance to the employee. Once accepted the employee may not withdraw the resignation without the employer's consent.

It is a good idea to ask the employee why he or she is leaving. Answers may alert the employer to potential problems with other employees. A written note of the employee's reasons for leaving should be kept.

If an employee resigns without giving notice he or she will be in breach of contract unless it is in response to a fundamental breach of contract by the employer (i.e. constructive dismissal). If the employee does resign without giving notice the employer can contractually require the employee to serve out the period of notice which he or she should have given, but in practice this would be very difficult to enforce because a court may not compel an employee to work. However, the employer should not pay the employee for any time after the date of resignation. The employee is not entitled to pay in lieu of the notice.

An employer may want an employee to serve out the correct period of notice to prevent the employee from immediately joining a competitor. A better way to do this may be to include a clause in the employee's contract restraining him or her (after leaving the employment) from working for a competitor. However, such restriction must be for a reasonable period of time only, and within a reasonable geographical distance from the former employer. Such clauses have to be carefully worded as the employee must be able to continue to earn a living. Such clauses shall only be enforceable if they are reasonably required for the protection of the employer's legitimate business interests. Alternatively or in addition, an employer may include what is known as a 'garden leave' clause in the contract of employment. Garden leave describes the situation where an employee serving their notice of termination is required to remain at home although they continue to be paid. The aim behind this practice is to prevent the employee from leaving to work for a competitor while not having that employee around at work where he or she may obtain confidential information. Employers wishing to include restrictive clauses or garden leave clauses in their contracts of employment should consult a solicitor.

(b) Redundancy – see page 89 for details

(c) Mutual agreement

The parties may mutually agree to terminate the contract of employment at any time. But if it is clear that the employee was forced to agree to the termination with the threat of dismissal, he or she will be held to have been unfair dismissed. Financial inducements to agree to terminate the employment are, however, fully acceptable.

If the parties mutually agree to end the contract, no notice of termination need be given by the employer. There will be no entitlement to pay in lieu of notice or redundancy pay. However it is fairly usual for the employer to make a payment described as an 'ex gratia payment' to avoid any implication of dismissal.

(d) Retirement

If an employer requires an employee to retire at a certain age, this should be included in the contract of employment. An employee may continue in employment beyond pensionable age for as long as he is able to work, unless there is an agreed upon retirement date or there is a recognised customary date for retirement in the trade or industry.

The right to complain of unfair dismissal and to claim a redundancy payment ceases when an employee reaches the normal retiring age of his or her employer or, if there is no normal retiring age, at the age of 65.

(e) Death

Unless a contract of employment provides otherwise, the death of either party terminates the contract.

Highlight
If the parties mutually agree to end the contract, no notice of termination need be given.

(f) Frustration

Very rarely, 'frustration' of a contract of employment occurs if some outside event happens that is not the fault of either party to the contract. The outside event must have been unforeseen by the parties when they entered into the contract and it must make it impossible for the contract to be performed at all, or it must make its performance radically different from its original purpose. If frustration occurs, the contract is terminated automatically without any need for either party to give notice.

Examples of frustration occurring are when an employee suffers an illness and as a result can never work again. Frustration may also occur if the employee is sentenced to prison.

In unfair dismissal cases employers have argued that there has been no dismissal but termination by frustration instead. It is not advisable to rely on frustration to avoid an unfair dismissal complaint, as employment tribunals do not readily accept that a contract has been terminated by frustration.

(g) Insolvency of the employer

Highlight
An employer's insolvency operates to terminate the contract of employment.

An employer's insolvency has the effect of terminating the contract of employment.

The employees may apply to the employer's representative for payment and if payment is not forthcoming, they may make an application to the Secretary of State for payment.

Claims and settlements for termination

In the preceding sections of this chapter reference has been made to claims of unfair dismissal, wrongful dismissal and redundancy payments. These are explored in further detail below to give employees an indication of their rights and employers an idea of potential liabilities and recommendations on how they might resolve these disputes.

Claims

(a) Unfair dismissal

Highlight
Dismissal of an employee without good reason or without following a fair procedure is likely to be unfair.

Dismissal of an employee without good reason, or without following a fair procedure, is likely to be unfair, liable to an unfair dismissal claim in an employment tribunal. The right not to be unfairly dismissed is a statutory right effective when the employment contract is entered into. It is subject to certain qualifying conditions.

Qualifying conditions

To bring a claim for unfair dismissal, an employee must currently have been employed under a contract for a minimum continuous period of one year from the commencement of the contract until the effective date of termination, and he or she must have been dismissed.

Continuity of employment remains unbroken even if there has been a transfer of business ownership, or employee absence from work because of sickness, injury, pregnancy or confinement (rules for assessing what is continuous employment are set out in sections 210 to 219 of the Employment Rights Act 1996).

The effective date of termination is either the date notice to terminate expires, the date of termination of employment or, if a fixed-term contract, the date on which it expires unrenewed. If the employer has not given the statutory minimum period of notice (except when entitled to dismiss without notice) the effective date of termination is the date when the statutory minimum period of notice to which the employee is entitled expires.

The time limit for bringing a claim for unfair dismissal is three months from the effective date of termination of the contract. An employment tribunal will extend the time limit when it is not practicable to bring the claim within this limit.

In most circumstances, no qualifying period of service is required if the dismissal is deemed to be automatically unfair. An employee who is dismissed on medical grounds specified in any health and safety at work law, regulation or code of practice can make a claim for unfair dismissal provided he or she has one month's continuous employment.

Excluded classes of employees

Certain employees are excluded from making a claim for unfair dismissal. They are:

- employees over normal retirement age or, if there is no retirement age, 65;

- employees working aboard (please note that this exception is due to be abolished under the Employment Relations Act 1999);

- in certain circumstances employees dismissed in connection with a strike, lock-out or other industrial action.

No contracting-out

Employers cannot exclude or waive an employee's right not to be unfairly dismissed. The inclusion of such a term in a contract of employment would have no legal effect, leaving the employee at liberty to bring a complaint of unfair dismissal in the employment tribunal.

There are exceptions to this principle, and an agreement that limits the right not to be unfairly dismissed is effective in the following circumstances:

- if the agreement is reached through a conciliation officer from ACAS (see page 91);

- if it is a valid compromise agreement (see page 91);

- if it is a fixed-term contract of one year or more, where dismissal consists of the expiry of the term without it being renewed, and the agreement to limit the right not to be unfairly dismissed has been recorded in writing prior to the expiry of the term.

Reasons for dismissal

If an employee can prove that he or she has all the qualifying conditions to bring a claim for unfair dismissal, the employer then has to establish the reason, or principal reason (if there was more than one), for the dismissal and prove it falls within one of the following acceptable reasons:

- connected to the capability or qualifications of the employee for performing work of the kind which he or she was employed to do; capability is assessed by reference to skill, aptitude, health or any other physical or mental quality (Appendices 25 and 26 are examples of dismissal letters for capability and sickness – where dismissal is for one of the other reasons, these letters can be adapted accordingly);

- connected to the conduct of the employee; or

- redundancy; or

- the employee could not continue to work in the position which he or she held without violating (either on his or her part or on that of his or her employer) a duty or restriction imposed by or under a law; or

- connected with some other substantial reason of a kind sufficient to justify the dismissal of an employee.

If the employer can satisfy the employment tribunal that the reason or principal reason for dismissal is one of the above, the tribunal will consider whether dismissal was fair or unfair. The tribunal will look at the reason given by the employer, all the circumstances surrounding the dismissal including the size and administrative resources of the employer, in order to decide the reasonableness of the dismissal. If the employment tribunal is not satisfied that dismissal was for an acceptable reason, dismissal shall be ruled unfair.

Test of reasonableness

The decisive factor at this stage is whether or not the employer followed a fair procedure, appropriate in the circumstances, leading up to the dismissal. This is why the practice of using standard, fair procedures for the various circumstances that arise during the employment relationship can be crucial to avoid liability for unfair dismissal. Different procedures are appropriate for the different circumstances. This Guide includes various procedure flowcharts in the Appendices for reference (see page 97).

Automatically unfair dismissals

Dismissal for any of the following reasons is automatically unfair:

- membership or non-membership of an independent trade union or taking part in activities of an independent trade union

- a maternity-related reason (see page 42)

- a health and safety reason

- asserting statutory rights

- performance by an employee representative (or candidate to be an employee representative)

- performance by an employee who is a pension scheme trustee

- on the transfer of an undertaking i.e. where the ownership of the employer is transferred from one person/entity to another

- refusal by a shop worker or betting worker - above or below retirement age - to work on a Sunday; such a worker refusing Sunday work also has the right not be subjected to a detriment

- a spent conviction or failure to disclose a spent conviction or

- unfair selection for redundancy i.e. selection will be unfair if it is for any of the above reasons

Note that it is only necessary for the employee to establish a period of continuous employment in the last two above situations. Also note that

Highlight
The tribunal will look at the reason given by the employer, all of the circumstances surrounding the dismissal including the size and administrative resources of the employer in order to decide the reasonableness of the dismissal.

with the forthcoming changes under the Employment Relations Act 1999, there will be other circumstances when dismissal will be automatically unfair; for example: dismissal for taking parental leave or taking time off for dependants, and performing functions as an employee representative (or as a candidate to be an employee representative) for the purposes of establishing a workforce agreement in relation to parental leave.

Remedies

If a tribunal finds that dismissal has been unfair it may make an order for reinstatement (for the employee to return to his or her original job), re-engagement (for the employee to be placed in employment comparable to that from which he or she was dismissed or other suitable employment) or compensation (up to a statutory maximum limit).

Compensation is the most common remedy and usually comprises a basic award and a compensatory award. Further details of these are set out below. In addition, there are further awards made in certain circumstances, such as an 'additional award' if the employer fails to comply with an order for re-instatement or re-engagement, and a 'special award' if the employer fails to comply with an order for re-instatement or re-engagement where dismissal was on the grounds of trade union membership or activities or health and safety duties. Please note however that special awards are due to be replaced by additional awards under the Employment Relations Act 1999.

(i) *Basic award*

The basic award is calculated by considering the employee's age, length of continuous service and gross average weekly wage. Each completed year of service up to a maximum of 20 counts for payment on the following scale (with a maximum of [currently] £220 for a week's pay):

- up to 22 years of age – $1/2$ week's pay;

- between 22 and up to 41 years of age – 1 week's pay;

- between 41 and up to 65 years of age – $1^{1}/2$ week's pay.

Where an employee is dismissed after his or her 64th birthday the basic award is reduced by one twelfth for every month after that.

The current maximum basic award is £6,600 (i.e. $1^{1}/2 \times 20 \times 220$).

A tribunal will reduce the basic award if it considers it is just and equitable to do so.

(ii) *Compensatory award*

The compensatory award is an amount the employment tribunal considers just and equitable, in all the circumstances relating to the loss sustained by the employee, as a result of the dismissal. The award is calculated on the net value of wages, other benefits and expenses reasonably incurred by the employee as a result of the dismissal.

Factors an employment tribunal will take into account to reduce the award are:

- contributory fault

- whether dismissal would have resulted even if the employer had acted reasonably

- the employee's duty to minimise his or her loss by attempting to seek other employment

- payments made by the employer

- what is just and equitable

Once the assessment of the compensatory award has been made, the statutory limit, which is currently £12,000 (except in cases of refusal to comply with a re-instatement or re-engagement order), must be applied. Please note the statutory limit is due to increase to £50,000 in/around October 1999 and annual increases on limits on all statutory awards and payments are due to be index-linked.

(b) Wrongful dismissal

Wrongful dismissal is a common law remedy distinct from unfair dismissal. It occurs when an employer terminates an employee's contract of employment in a way that breaches it or the employer's conduct is such that it entitles the employee to resign (i.e. constructive dismissal). In these circumstances the employee may take proceedings against the employer in an employment tribunal or in the civil courts (County Court or the High Court) for wrongful dismissal claiming damages for breach of contract. There is no requirement for the employee to have a qualifying period of continuous employment to make such a claim.

Damages are assessed on the basis that they should put the employee in the position he or she would have been in had the contract been performed in accordance with its terms. This is subject to a duty of the employee to mitigate his or her loss (e.g. minimising his or her loss by seeking other employment). Damages for wrongful dismissal are usually assessed by reference to the period of notice by which the employer could lawfully have terminated the contract. However, if the

Highlight
The compensatory award is calculated on the net value of wages, other benefits and expenses reasonably incurred by the employee as a result of the dismissal.

employee has been dismissed in breach of a contractual disciplinary procedure, the damages may be assessed with reference to the time that it would have taken to go through the disciplinary procedure.

Employees are not entitled to damages for loss, injury to feelings or distress arising from the manner of dismissal, and generally nor are they entitled to damages for injury to reputation. However, recent case law has concluded that if an employer has damaged the employee's chance of obtaining further employment through loss of reputation, he may also be liable to compensate for continuing financial loss which the employee suffers as a result.

(c) Redundancy

Employees in a redundancy situation are entitled to a statutory redundancy payment. Also, if dismissal by reason of redundancy is not effected in a reasonable way, it may amount to unfair dismissal.

Definition of a redundancy situation

A redundancy situation exists where an employee's dismissal was attributable wholly or mainly to the fact that:

- the employer has ceased, or intends to cease, to carry on the business for which the employee was employed or has ceased, or intends to cease, to carry it on at a place where the employee was employed (i.e. relocation); or

- the business's need for work for which employees were taken on has, or is expected to, cease or diminish (i.e. reduction in the number of employees required).

Statutory redundancy payment

Employees in a redundancy situation are entitled to a statutory redundancy payment if they have at least two years' service after reaching the age of 18. The entitlement is calculated in the same way as the basic award for unfair dismissal claims (except employment prior to reaching 18 is not counted). The calculation is made by considering the employee's age, length of continuous service and gross average weekly wage. Each completed year of service, up to a maximum of 20 after the age of 18, counts for payment on the following scale (with a maximum of [currently] £220 for a week's pay):

- between 18 and up to 22 years of age – ¹/₂ week's pay;

- between 22 and up to 41 years of age – 1 week's pay;

- between 41 and up to 65 years of age – 1¹/₂ weeks' pay.

Where an employee is made redundant after his or her 64th birthday the payment is reduced by one-twelfth for every month after that.

The current maximum redundancy payment is £6,600 (i.e. $1^1/_2 \times 20 \times 220$).

An employee may raise a complaint with an employment tribunal if he or she has not received the correct redundancy payment. The time limit for such a claim is six months from the relevant date as defined by Section 145 of the Employment Rights Act 1996 (usually the effective date of termination). The time limit may be extended for a further six months if approved by the employment tribunal.

An employee is not entitled to statutory redundancy payment if, before existing employment ends, the employer offers him or her (orally or in writing), employment on the same terms or suitable alternative employment, to commence within 4 weeks of the ending of the original employment. If the employee unreasonably refuses such an offer, or during a trial period for the new job unreasonably terminates such employment, he or she loses the right to statutory redundancy payment.

If the employee leaves employment before dismissal takes effect, and the employer objects in writing, the employment tribunal may determine the extent of the employee's entitlement.

Unfair dismissal

Dismissal for redundancy may be unfair, by a failure by the employer to comply with the obligation to consult with appropriate representatives of the employees concerned. These are either representatives of an independent trade union or other elected representatives. Failure to adhere to an agreed redundancy procedure does not render a dismissal automatically unfair, but may be relevant to the tribunal's view of the procedure actually adopted by the employer (see Appendix 24).

The amount of a basic award will be reduced by the amount of any redundancy payment awarded by a tribunal or paid by the employer in respect of the same dismissal.

Highlight
An employee may raise a complaint with an employment tribunal if he or she has not received the correct amount of redundancy payment.

Highlight
Failure to adhere to an agreed redundancy procedure does not render a dismissal automatically unfair but may be relevant to the tribunal's view of the procedure actually adopted by the employer.

Settlements

Where there is a dispute, the parties will often prefer to settle the matter rather than proceed to a hearing. A settlement agreement is only binding if either of the following courses are taken:

(a) ACAS conciliation

One way to contract out validly of an employee's right to pursue a case to a tribunal is by means of a settlement promoted by an ACAS conciliation officer (see Appendix 18). A conciliation officer has a duty to promote a settlement once a complaint has been put to a tribunal if requested to do so by the complainant, the employee concerned, or if in the absence of such request, the conciliation officer considers there is a reasonable prospect of achieving a settlement.

Settlements are recorded on ACAS form COT 3, signed by the parties and contain a clause under which the complainant agrees that no further proceedings arising out of the matter will be pursued by him or her.

(b) Compromise agreements

The only other way to settle a matter validly is by making a compromise agreement between the parties.

For a compromise agreement to be effective, it must be in writing and must fulfil the following conditions:

- it must relate to the particular complaint (it is therefore not possible to simply have a clause stating that the agreement is in full and final settlement of all claims that the ex-employee has or may have against the employer);

- the employee must have received independent legal advice from a qualified lawyer, an officer of an independent trade union or a worker at an advice centre as to the terms and effect of the proposed agreement, and in particular its effects on his or her ability to pursue the appropriate rights before an employment tribunal. The advisor who gives the advice must have an insurance policy covering the risk of a claim by the employee for an alleged loss arising out of the advice;

- the agreement must identify the advisor;

- the agreement must declare that the above conditions are satisfied.

If none of these courses is taken the employee shall still be at liberty to commence proceedings despite the fact that he or she has received a compensation payment to settle. If he or she does proceed to make a claim however, the payment can be taken into account when assessing compensation.

However, if the dispute is only in relation to wrongful dismissal, (i.e. it is only a contractual claim), the parties may settle validly by agreement without the need for any special requirements to be satisfied. You will find basic example compromise agreements for unfair dismissal and redundancy at Appendices 28 and 29.

Glossary
of useful terms

A - C

ACAS – Advisory, Conciliation and Arbitration Service. Established under the Employment Protection Act 1975; now consolidated into the Trade Union and Labour Relations (Consolidation) Act 1992.

Action in good faith – an act carried out honestly.

Agent – a person appointed by another to act on his behalf.

Applicant – someone who lodges a complaint with an employment tribunal.

Augment – to supplement.

Breach of contract – a failure by a party of a contract to live up to the terms agreed to in the contract or to perform the obligations delineated in the contract.

Civil wrong – a non-criminal wrong based on denial of another person's rights.

Code of practice – rules established by regulatory, administrative bodies, trade associations, etc., which are used to suggest and guide behaviour. These rules do not have the force of law.

Collective agreement – agreement reached as a result of negotiations between an employer and a trade union.

Common law – laws arising from court rulings rather than from legislative enactments.

Complainant – someone who lodges a complaint.

Constructive dismissal – resignation by an employee in circumstances such that he or she is entitled to resign by reason of an act, or course of action by the employer.

Contract for service – a type of contract that defines an independent contractor.

Contract of service – a type of contract in which a person agrees to be paid a regular wage, work regular hours, and consider himself an employee.

C- R ════════════════════════════════

Contract out – attempting to exclude or limit liability.

DDA – Disability Discrimination Act 1996. Prohibits discrimination based on disability relating to employment and access to goods, facilities, services and premises.

Discrimination – treatment of one or more members of a specified group in a manner that is unfair as compared to the treatment of other people who are not members of that group.

EPA – Equal Pay Act 1970. Requires that men and women be paid the same rate for like employment, or work rated as equivalent or having equal value.

Ex gratia – given as a favour. An ex gratia payment is one not required to be made by a legal duty.

Express terms – the terms and provisions of a contract that the parties specifically deal with and agree upon.

Guarantee payments – the sum that an employer must pay an employee for whom he is unable to provide work, under the Employment Rights Act 1996.

Frustration – an unexpected and unintentional event that makes the fulfilment of the terms of a contract impossible.

Gross wages – the amount of wages before any deductions are made.

Implied terms – terms that are not expressly stated in a contract but are necessary to give it business efficacy or are derived from custom and usage.

Indemnification – one person agrees to pay to a third person money owed to him by a second person.

Legitimate interests – an employer's right to have certain interests protected by law.

Mandate – a legal order to do something.

Net wages – the amount of wages after deductions are made.

Notice – formal advance notification by either party to an employment contract, to the other, that the contract is about to expire and will not be renewed.

PIW – Period of Incapacity for Work. Any period of four or more consecutive days during which the employee has been found incapable of working due to illness.

Redundancy – termination of employment because a job no longer exists.

R – W

Remuneration – reward or pay for service

Repudiatory breach – a fundamental breach of contract by either the employer or the employee that entitles the other party to terminate the relationship without giving notice.

Respondent – the person against whom relief is sought by the applicant.

Restrictive covenant – a provision in a contract prohibiting certain post-employment activities on the part of an ex-employee.

RRA – Race Relations Act 1976. Prohibits discrimination based on colour, race, nationality, or ethnic or national origin in employment, services and housing.

SDA – Sex Discrimination Act 1975. Prohibits discrimination based on gender or marital status in employment, or when offering a contract of employment.

SMP – Statutory Maternity Pay. An employer must pay SMP to any employee who is eligible.

Share fishing – a work structure amongst fishermen whereby they rotate shifts and share a boat.

Spent conviction – a conviction that, after a specified period of time, can be treated as if it never existed, and does not need to be disclosed.

SSP – Statutory Sick Pay. An employer must pay SSP to any employee who is out ill after the first four days of absence, up to 28 weeks.

Statement of particulars – for a written statement outlining the nature, terms, duties and responsibilities of a specific job.

Statutory rights – any privilege recognised and protected by law.

Unfair dismissal – a remedy for unjustifiable dismissal based on statutory rights.

Winding up – a procedure by which a company liquidates its assets and dissolves itself.

Wrongful dismissal – a remedy for unjustifiable dismissal based on contractual rights.

Appendices

Sentence	Rehabilitation Periods
Imprisonment, corrective training or sentence of detention in a young offenders' institution for between 6 and 30 months	10 years
Imprisonment or sentence of detention in a young offenders' institution for a term not exceeding 6 months	7 years
A fine or the sentence not expressly covered by the Rehabilitation of Offenders Act 1974	5 years
Order for detention in a detention centre	3 years
Absolute discharge	6 months
Conditional discharge	1 year
Probation	5 years

NB For young offenders, periods are usually reduced by half, except in cases of probation

APPENDIX 2
Documents as evidence of entitlements to work in the UK

- Any document containing the National Insurance number of the person named in a document issued by the:

  Inland Revenue
  Benefits Agency
  Contributions Agency
  Employment Service

- A passport stating the holder to be a British citizen:

  having the right to live in the UK
  having an entitlement to re-enter the UK

- A passport issued by, or on behalf of, the UK Government containing a Certificate of Entitlement to live in the UK.

- A certificate for Registration of Naturalisation as a British citizen.

- A Birth Certificate issued in the UK, the Republic of Ireland, the Channel Islands or the Isle of Man.

- A passport or national identity card which describes the holder as a National of the State issuing the documents, that State being a party to the European Economic Area Agreement.

- A passport or other travel document or letter from the Home Office stating that the holder is exempt from immigration control or has indefinite leave to enter or remain in the UK, or has no time limit to stay.

- A passport or other travel document or letter from the Home Office stating that the holder has current leave to enter or remain in the UK and is not precluded from taking the employment in question.

- A UK residence permit held by a European National.

- A passport or other travel document stating that the holder has a current right of residence in the UK by virtue of being a family member of a named European National in the UK.

- A letter from the Home Office stating that the named person is a British citizen or has permission to take up employment.

- A work permit or other document permitting employment issued by the Department for Education and Employment or the Training and Employment Agency or the Training and Employment Agency (Northern Ireland) or the Northern Ireland Social Security Agency.

- A passport stating that the holder is a British Dependant Territories citizen by virtue of a connection with Gibraltar.

Ace Fabrics Limited

Unit 2 Boxwood Trading Estate, Kings Langley, HO3 2HT
Tel: (01234) 456789 Fax: (01234) 987654 E-mail: ace@fab.comp

Miss S Porter
12 Elm Drive
MILTON KEYNES
ME9 427

25th July 1999

Dear *Miss Porter*

Thank you for sending me your application for the post of *Machinist*.

I would very much like to discuss this matter further with you and have arranged an interview at *10 am* on *Tuesday 6 August 1999* at these offices. I should be grateful if you would confirm your attendance.

I look forward to meeting you.

Yours sincerely

John Smith

John Smith
Personnel Manager

Registered Office: Unit 2 Boxwood Trading Estate, Kings Langley, HO3 2HT
Registered in England no 123 4567

Ace Fabrics Limited

Unit 2 Boxwood Trading Estate, Kings Langley, HO3 2HT
Tel: (01234) 456789 Fax: (01234) 987654 E-mail: ace@fab.comp

Miss S Porter
12 Elm Drive
MILTON KEYNES
ME9 427

25th July 1999

Dear *Miss Porter*

I refer to your application for the post of *Machinist* with this company.

I regret that after careful consideration you have not been selected for interview on this occasion as there were other applicants whose experience and qualifications matched our requirements more closely.

However, I would like to take this opportunity to thank you for your interest in our company and I should like to wish you every success in your future job hunting.

Yours sincerely

John Smith

John Smith
Personnel Manager

Registered Office: Unit 2 Boxwood Trading Estate, Kings Langley, HO3 2HT
Registered in England no 123 4567

Ace Fabrics Limited

Unit 2 Boxwood Trading Estate, Kings Langley, HO3 2HT
Tel: (01234) 456789   Fax: (01234) 987654   E-mail: ace@fab.comp

Dear *Miss Porter*

Post of *Machinist*

Following your interview at this office on *Tuesday 6 August 1999* I am pleased to offer you the above position with *Ace Fabrics Limited* ("the Company") subject to satisfactory references[1] and a medical report.[2] It is the Company's final decision as to whether such references meet with its requirements. You are advised not to resign from your present position until I have confirmed to you that your references have been received and are satisfactory to us. We will endeavour to obtain your references as quickly as possible.

If you accept this offer of employment, your job will be based at *Unit 2, Boxwood Trading Estate, Kings Langley, HO3 2HT.*

Your employment will commence on *Monday 2 September 1999* and the first four weeks will be treated as a probationary period during which time your employment may be terminated by yourself or by the Company on one week's notice.

Your duties and responsibilities will be as set out in the attached job description and you will be responsible to *Mr Brown.*

Your basic salary at the commencement of your employment will be *£14,500 per year* payable monthly in arrears by bank credit transfer on the last day of each month. Your normal weekly hours will be from *9 am to 5 pm Monday to Friday with one hour break for lunch.*

You will be entitled to *4 weeks* holiday in every year, in addition to the normal statutory entitlement, of which no more than *two* weeks may be taken consecutively. The holiday year runs from *1 February to 31 January.*

Continued.......

Registered Office: Unit 2 Boxwood Trading Estate, Kings Langley, HO3 2HT
Registered in England no 123 4567

[1] References are usually taken up at this stage, the offer being made subject to satisfactory references. See model letter of Request for Reference and footnotes at Appendix 6. A candidate who receives a job offer subject to satisfactory references should not resign from their current employment until all the conditions have been satisfied. In the public sector offers are usually made unconditional only after all conditions are met.

[2] Medical examinations of prospective employees are not a legal requirement although employers are recommended to carry them out now that health and safety in the workplace is so important. A prospective employee is not obliged to agree to have a medical examination although if they did refuse it would be reasonable for the prospective employer not to make an offer.

The Company will be entitled to terminate your appointment by giving you written notice of *one week for the first two years of service plus one week for every further year of service up to a maximum of twelve weeks.*

You are required to give the Company *one* week's notice of your intention to terminate your employment with the Company.

Your other terms of employment will be provided on your first day of employment.[3]

If you wish to accept this offer of employment I would be grateful if you could confirm your acceptance by signing and returning one copy of this letter in the stamped addressed envelope enclosed.[4]

I do hope that you will accept this offer. In the meantime, if you wish to discuss any aspect of this offer, please do not hesitate to contact me.

Yours sincerely

John Smith

John Smith
Personnel Manager

Registered Office: Unit 2 Boxwood Trading Estate, Kings Langley, HO3 2HT
Registered in England no 123 4567

[3] Alternatively, these may be set out in an enclosed statement of particulars of employment or incorporated into this letter.

[4] Once this offer has been accepted the parties have entered into a contractual relationship and the employer will need to issue either a full contract or a statement of particulars of employment (see chapter 2).

Ace Fabrics Limited

Unit 2 Boxwood Trading Estate, Kings Langley, HO3 2HT
Tel: (01234) 456789 Fax: (01234) 987654 E-mail: ace@fab.comp

Dear Sir

Re: Miss Porter

The above named has applied to us for the position of *Machinist* and has given us your name as a referee.[2]

We understand that *Miss Porter* was employed by you from *2 January 1991 to 2 August 1999* as a *machinist*. We should be grateful if you would confirm that this is the case and let us know whether in your opinion she performed her tasks competently and conscientiously.

We should also be grateful if you would let us know whether you would consider *Miss Porter* a reliable and responsible employee. Could you also let us know the reasons why she left your employment?

In order that we can comply with our obligations to provide statutory parental leave, please inform us if *Miss Porter* has taken any parental leave, and if so, how much time has been taken.[3]

We assure you that any reply that you may give will be treated in the strictest confidence.[4]

A stamped addressed envelope is enclosed.[5]

Yours faithfully[6]

John Smith

John Smith
Personnel Manager

Registered Office: Unit 2 Boxwood Trading Estate, Kings Langley, HO3 2HT
Registered in England no 123 4567

---

[1] There is no legal obligation to provide a reference although it is rare that an employer or ex-employer will refuse to supply one. If a reference is given, it should be accurate. If it is not accurate the person who gives the reference may be liable to an action for: *(a)* **defamation** by the subject if the inaccuracy damages the reputation of the subject. The person who gives the reference will not be liable for defamation if they believe the information to be correct and gives it without malice; *(b)* **negligence** by both the subject and the recipient, both of whom could sue for damages for any financial loss arising out of a negligent reference. Wording may be included in the reference to exclude legal liability as in the model reference letter at Appendix 8.

[2] The request may be for a reference to be given over the telephone and sometimes employers or ex-employers are more willing to give fuller information than in writing. Again, there is no legal obligation to give a reference over the telephone but if it is given, it should be accurate.

[3] This should be asked of all applicants, both female and male.

[4] All references should be marked 'private and confidential'.

[5] It is customary to include a stamped address envelope for the return reference. The advantage of this is that the reference is returned straight to the person for whom it is intended.

[6] In addition to obtaining references a potential employer is advised to check the prospective employee's qualifications, if possible before the job offer is made.

Ace Fabrics Limited

Unit 2 Boxwood Trading Estate, Kings Langley, HO3 2HT
Tel: (01234) 456789 Fax: (01234) 987654 E-mail: ace@fab.comp

Dear *Miss Porter,*

Thank you for attending the interview for the post of *Machinist* at this office on *Tuesday 6 August 1999.*

I regret that after careful consideration your application has been unsuccessful on this occasion as there were candidates whose qualifications and experience matched our requirements more closely.

However, I would like to take this opportunity to thank you for your interest in our company and I should also like to wish you every success in finding a suitable post in the near future.

Yours sincerely

John Smith

John Smith
Personnel Manager

Registered Office: Unit 2 Boxwood Trading Estate, Kings Langley, HO3 2HT
Registered in England no 123 4567

---

[1] It is a good idea to wait until the preferred candidate has accepted the offer before sending the letters of rejection to the other candidates. Subject to this, it is good practice to notify unsuccessful candidates as soon as possible.

Fabric Works Limited
Unit 17 Felsham Trading Estate
Bovingdon HP17 2LS
Tel: (01987) 789456
Fax: (01987) 654987

Dear *Mr. Smith*,

Re: *Miss Porter*

In reply to your request for a reference for the above named, I confirm that *Miss Porter* was employed by this Company between the dates of *2 January 1991 and 2 August 1999* as a *machinist*.

During her employment with this Company *Miss Porter* performed her tasks competently and conscientiously and I consider her to be a reliable and responsible employee. *Miss Porter* left our employment due to redundancy.

This reference is given to be of help to you and in fairness to your proposed employee. It is given on the basis that we accept no legal liability and that you must rely upon your own judgement whether or not to proceed with your proposed employment of this individual. We trust you shall hold this reference in strict confidence.

Yours sincerely

Peter Johnson

Peter Johnson
Managing Director

Registered Office: Unit 17 Felsham Trading Estate Bovingdon HP17 2LS
Registered in England no 123 9876

Information which must be included in the principal statement:

- the names of the parties;

- the date on which employment began and the date on which any previous employment (with this or any other employer) commenced which is to be regarded as continuous with this employment;

- the scale or rate of remuneration or the method of calculating such remuneration and the frequency of payment;

- any terms and conditions relating to hours or work, including normal working hours;

- any terms and conditions relating to entitlement to holidays, including public holidays and holiday pay (sufficient to enable the employee's entitlement, including entitlement to accrued holiday pay on termination, to be precisely calculated);

- the employee's job title or a brief description of his or her work;

- the employee's place of work, or where the employee is required or permitted to work at various places, an indication of that fact, together with the address of the employer.

Information which must be given in writing (but which may or may not be included in the principal statement):

- where the employment is not intended to be permanent, the period for which it is expected to continue;

- where the employment is for a fixed term, the expiry date;

- the length of notice the employee is obliged to give and is entitled to receive in order to terminate his or her contract (or reference to the law or an accessible collective agreement);

- rules relating to sick leave, and sick pay (or reference to a document where such details may be found);

- any collective agreements which directly affect the employee's terms and conditions of employment including, where the employer is not a party, the names of the parties;

- details of any pensions or pension schemes (or reference to documents where such details may be found);

- a statement of whether a contracting-out certificate is or is not in force;

- where the employee is required to work outside the United Kingdom for more than one month, the period of such service, the currency in which remuneration will be paid, and additional remuneration and/or benefits provided while working overseas and any terms and conditions of employment relating to the employee's return to the United Kingdom;

- any disciplinary rules and grievance procedures applying to the employee (or reference to documents where such details may be found). This only applies to the employer who employs over 20 employees;

- the persons to whom the employee can apply for redress of any grievances or dissatisfaction with a disciplinary decision (or reference to documents where such details may be found).

Where there are no terms to be given under any of these headings, this should be stated.

<u>EMPLOYMENT CONTRACT</u>

THIS AGREEMENT IS MADE the *20th day of August 1999.*[1]

BETWEEN (1) *Ace Fabrics Limited of Unit 2, Boxwood Trading Estate, Kings Langley HO3 2HT* (the "Employer") and (2) *Susan Porter of 12 Elm Drive, Milton Keynes ME9 427* (the "Employee")

This document sets out the terms and conditions of employment which are required to be given to the Employee under Section 1 Employment Rights Act 1996[2] and which apply at the date hereof.

1.   COMMENCEMENT AND JOB TITLE

The Employer agrees to employ the Employee from *2nd September 1999* in the capacity of *Machinist* at *Unit 2, Boxwood Trading Estate.* No employment with a previous employer will be counted as part of the Employee's period of continuous employment[3]. The Employee's duties which this job entails are set out in the job description attached to this statement. The job description may from time to time be reasonably modified as necessary to meet the needs of the Employer's business.

2.   SALARY

The Employer shall pay the Employee a salary of *£14,500* per year payable by credit transfer at monthly intervals on the last day of each month. The Company shall review the Employee's salary at such intervals as it shall at its sole discretion decide.

3.   HOURS OF EMPLOYMENT

The Employee's normal hours of employment shall be *9.00 am* to *5.00 pm* on *Mondays* to *Fridays* during which time the Employee may take up to one hour for lunch between the hours of *12.00 pm and 2.00 pm*, and the Employee may from time to time be required to work such additional hours as is reasonable to meet the requirements of the Employer's business at an overtime rate of *£7.50* per hour.

4.   HOLIDAYS

The Employee shall be entitled to *20* days' holiday per calendar year at full pay in addition to the normal public holidays. Holidays must be taken at times convenient to the Employer and sufficient notice of intention to take holiday must be given to the Employee's supervisor. No more than 2 weeks' holiday must be taken at any one time unless permission is given by *the Employee's* supervisor. Holiday untaken in the calendar year to which it relates will be lost and may not be carried forward.

The Employee shall be entitled to payment in lieu of holiday accrued due but untaken at the date of termination of his or her employment. If at the date of termination the Employee has taken holiday in excess of his or her accrued entitlement a corresponding deduction will be made from his or her final payment.

---

[1] This must be no later than two months after the employment commences. Any changes must be notified to the employee within one month of the change. No statement is required to be given to an employee employed under a contract for less than one month.

[2] For agreements entered into prior to 22 August 1996 the Employment Protection (Consolidation) Act 1978 applies.

[3] If employment with a previous employer is to be counted as a period of continuous employment this, and the date it began, must be stated.

5. SICKNESS

5.1 If the Employee is absent from work on account of sickness or injury, he or she or someone on his or her behalf should inform the Employer of the reason for the absence as soon as possible but no later than *12.00 pm* on the working day on which absence first occurs.

5.2 *The Company reserves the right to ask the Employee at any stage of absence to produce a medical certificate and/or to undergo a medical examination.*

5.3 The Employee shall be paid normal remuneration during sickness absence for a maximum of *4 weeks* in any period of *12 months* provided that the Employee provides the Employer with a medical certificate in the case of absence of more than *7 consecutive days*. Such remuneration will be less the amount of any Statutory Sick Pay or Social Security sickness benefits to which the Employee may be entitled. Entitlement to payment is subject to notification of absence and production of medical certificates as required above.[4]

6. COLLECTIVE AGREEMENTS

There are no collective agreements in force directly relating to the terms of your employment.[5]

7. PENSION

The Employee shall be entitled to join the Employer's pension scheme, the details of which are set out in the Employer's booklet/leaflet which is entitled *Your Pension at Ace Fabrics* and which is available on request. A contracting-out certificate under the Pension Schemes Act 1993 is in force in respect of this employment.[6]

8. TERMINATION

The Employer may terminate this Agreement by giving written notice to the Employee as follows:

(a) With not less than one week's notice during the first two years of continuous employment; then

(b) With not less than a further one week's notice for each full year of continuous employment after the first two years until the 12th year of continuous employment; and

(c) With not less than 12 weeks' notice after 12 years of continuous employment.[7]

The Employer may terminate this Agreement without notice or payment in lieu of notice in the case of serious or persistent misconduct such as to cause a major breach of the Employer's disciplinary rules.

The Employee may terminate this Agreement by one week's written notice to the Employer.

After notice of termination has been given by either party, provided the Employee continues to be paid and to enjoy his or her full contractual benefits under the terms of this Agreement, the Employer may in its absolute discretion for all or part of the notice period exclude the Employee from the premises of the Employer and require that he or she carries out duties other than those specified in his or her job description or require that he or she carries out no duties at all until the termination of his or her employment.

---

[4] If the employer does not wish to pay normal remuneration during sickness they should state that the statutory sick pay rules apply.

[5] Where a collective agreement directly affects the terms and conditions of employment the following should be inserted as clause 6: 'The terms of the collective agreement dated [ ] made between [ ] and [ ] shall deemed to be included in this agreement'.

9. CONFIDENTIALITY

The Employee is aware that during his or her employment he or she may be party to confidential information concerning the Employer and the Employer's business. The Employee shall not during the term of his or her employment disclose or allow the disclosure of any confidential information (except in the proper course of his or her employment).

After the termination of this Agreement the Employee shall not disclose or use any of the Employer's trade secrets or any other information which is of a sufficiently high degree of confidentiality to amount to a trade secret. The Employer shall be entitled to apply for an injunction to prevent such disclosure or use and to seek any other remedy including without limitation the recovery of damages in the case of such disclosure or use.

10. NON-COMPETITION

For a period of *six months*[8] after the termination of this Agreement the Employee shall not solicit or seek business from any customers or clients of the Employer who were customers or clients of the Employer at the time during the *12 months*[9] immediately preceding the termination of this Agreement.

11. DISCIPLINE AND GRIEVANCE

The Employer's disciplinary rules and procedure and the grievance and appeal procedure in connection with these rules are set out in the Employer's leaflets entitled *Disciplinary Rules and Procedure at Ace Fabrics Limited* and *Grievance Procedure at Ace Fabrics Limited* respectively which are attached hereto.[10]

12. NOTICES

All communications including notices required to be given under this Agreement shall be in writing and shall be sent either by personal service or first class post to the parties' respective addresses.

13. SEVERABILITY

If any provision of this Agreement should be held to be invalid it shall to that extent be severed and the remaining provisions shall continue to have full force and effect.

14. STAFF HANDBOOK

Further details of the arrangements affecting your employment are published in the *Staff Handbook* as issued from time to time. These are largely of an administrative nature but, so far as relevant, are to be treated as incorporated in this Agreement.

[6] Where no pension scheme exists this must be stated and where no contracting out certificate is in force this must also be stated.

[7] These are minimum periods required by law but they may be increased by agreement.

[8] The employer may choose any number of months or years but any more than two years is likely to render this clause unenforceable at law. Also see note on terms in restraint of trade on page 35.

[9] This period should be between one and three years if it is to remain enforceable by the employer.

[10] See Appendices 11 and 12

15.   GOVERNING LAW

This Agreement shall be construed in accordance with the laws of England and Wales and shall be subject to the exclusive jurisdiction of the English Courts.

Please acknowledge receipt of this statement and your agreement to the terms set out in it by signing the attached copy of this letter and returning it to *Mr Smith*.

IN WITNESS OF WHICH the parties hereto have signed this Agreement the day and year first above written.

SIGNED   _____   _____

Signed by or on behalf of *Ace Fabrics Ltd*   in the presence of (witness)

Name _____

Address _____

_____

DATED _____   Occupation _____

SIGNED   _____   _____

Signed by the Employee   in the presence of (witness)

Name _____

Address _____

_____

DATED _____   Occupation _____

DISCIPLINARY RULES AND PROCEDURE *AT ACE FABRICS LIMITED*

1. The Company's aim is to encourage improvement in individual performance and conduct. Employees are required to treat members of the public and other employees equally in accordance with the Equal Opportunities Policy.[1] This procedure sets out the action which will be taken when disciplinary rules are breached.

2. Principles:

    (i)   The list of rules is not to be regarded as an exhaustive list.

    (ii)   The procedure is designed to establish the facts quickly and to deal consistently with disciplinary issues. No disciplinary action will be taken until the matter has been fully investigated.

    (iii) At every stage employees will have the opportunity to state their case and be accompanied by a fellow employee of their choice at the hearings.

    (iv)   Only a Director has the right to suspend or dismiss. An employee may, however, be given a verbal or written warning by their immediate superior.

    (v)   An employee has the right to appeal against any disciplinary decision.

3. The Rules:

    Breaches of the Company's disciplinary rules which can lead to disciplinary action are:

    *   failure to observe a reasonable order or instruction;

    *   failure to observe a health and safety requirement;

    *   inadequate time keeping;

    *   absence from work without proper cause (including taking parental leave dishonestly);

    *   theft or removal of the Company's property;

    *   loss, damage to or misuse of the Company's property through negligence or carelessness;

    *   conduct detrimental to the interests of the Company;

    *   incapacity for work due to being under the influence of alcohol or illegal drugs;

    *   physical assault or gross insubordination;

    *   committing an act outside work or being convicted for a criminal offence which is liable adversely to affect the performance of the contract of employment and/or the relationship between the employee and the Company;

    *   failure to comply with the Company's Equal Opportunities Policy.

---

[1] See Appendix 17.

4. The Procedure:

    (i) Oral warning

        If conduct or performance is unsatisfactory, the employee will be given a formal oral warning, which will be recorded. The warning will be disregarded after six months' satisfactory service.

    (ii) Written warning

        If the offence is serious, if there is no improvement in standards, or if a further offence occurs, a written warning will be given which will include the reason for the warning and a note that, if there is no improvement after twelve months, a final written warning will be given.

    (iii) Final written warning

        If conduct or performance is still unsatisfactory, or if a further serious offence occurs within the 12-month period, a final written warning will be given making it clear that any recurrence of the offence or other serious misconduct within a period of one month will result in dismissal.

    (iv) Dismissal

        If there is no satisfactory improvement or if further serious misconduct occurs, the employee will be dismissed.

    (v) Gross misconduct

        If, after investigation, it is confirmed that an employee has committed an offence of the following nature (the list is not exhaustive) the normal consequence will be dismissal:

        •   theft of or damage to the Company's property, incapacity for work due to being under the influence of alcohol or illegal drugs, physical assault and gross insubordination, discrimination or harassment contrary to the Company's Equal Opportunities Policy.

        While the alleged gross misconduct is being investigated the employee may be suspended, during which time he or she will be paid the normal hourly rate. Any decision to dismiss will be taken by the employer only after a full investigation.

    (vi) Appeals

        An employee who wishes to appeal against any disciplinary decision must do so to *Mr. Jones* within two working days. The employer will hear the appeal and decide the case as impartially as possible.

GRIEVANCE PROCEDURE AT *ACE FABRICS LIMITED*

1.   The following procedure shall be applied to settle all disputes or grievances concerning an employee or employees of the Company (but excluding those relating to redundancy selection).

2.   Principles:

   (i)   It is the intention of both parties that employees should be encouraged to have direct contact with management to resolve their problems.

   (ii)   The procedure for resolution of grievances and avoidance of disputes is available if the parties are unable to agree a solution to a problem.

   (iii)   Should a matter be referred to this procedure for resolution, both parties should accept that it should be progressed as speedily as possible, with a joint commitment that every effort will be made to ensure that such a reference takes no longer than seven working days to complete.

   (iv)   Pending resolution of the grievance, the same conditions prior to its notification shall continue to apply, except in those circumstances where such a continuation would have damaging effects upon the Company's business.

   (v)   It is agreed between the parties that where the grievance is of a collective nature, i.e. affecting more than one employee, it shall be referred initially to (ii) of the procedure.

   (vi)   If the employee's immediate supervisor/manager is the subject of the grievance and for this reason the employee does not wish the grievance to be heard by him or her, it shall be referred initially to (ii) of the procedure.

3.   The Procedure:

   (i)   Where an employee has a grievance, he shall raise the matter with his or her immediate supervisor/manager.

   (ii)   If the matter has not been resolved at (i), it shall be referred to a more senior manager or director and the shop steward, full time trade union officer, or fellow employee, if requested shall be present. A statement summarising the main details of the grievance and the reasons for the failure to agree must be prepared and signed by both parties.

   (iii)   In the event of a failure to agree, the parties will consider whether conciliation or arbitration is appropriate. The Company may refer the dispute to the Advisory Conciliation and Arbitration Service, whose findings may, by mutual prior agreement, be binding on both parties.

A ce F abrics L imited

Unit 2 Boxwood Trading Estate, Kings Langley, HO3 2HT
Tel: (01234) 456789 Fax: (01234) 987654 E-mail: ace@fab.comp

Miss S Porter
12 Elm Drive
MILTON KEYNES
ME9 427

11 December 1999

Dear Miss Porter

I refer to our meeting on 12 December 1999.

As I explained at that meeting, we regret that because of economic pressure we have no option but to lay you off from work.

The period of lay off shall take effect from 20 December 1999 and shall continue until 20 January 2000. You shall receive guarantee payments of £15.35 per day for the first five days of this period.

I very much regret that we have been forced to take this action, but I should like to assure you that we are working hard to ensure that the period of lay off is kept to a minimum.

Yours sincerely

John Smith

John Smith
Personnel Manager

Registered Office: Unit 2 Boxwood Trading Estate, Kings Langley, HO3 2HT
Registered in England no 123 4567

[1] See page 26 for an explanation of the rules relating to employees being laid off and guarantee payments.

As a justice of the peace.

As a member of a local authority.

As a member of the Broads Authority[1].

As a member of any statutory tribunal.

As a member of a board of visitors or a visiting committee.

As a member of a National Health Service trust, a Regional Health Authority, an Area Health Authority, a District Health Authority, a Family Practitioner Committee or a Health Board.

As a member of the managing or governing body of an educational establishment maintained by a local education authority or a school council or the governing body of a designated institution or a central institution.

As a member of the governing body of a grant-maintained school.

As a member of the governing body of a further education corporation or higher education corporation.

As a member of a school board or of the board of management of a self-governing school.

As a member of the board of management of a college of further education.

As a member of the National Rivers Authority or a river purification board.

[1] An authority with responsibilities for conservation and recreation on the Norfolk Broads.

Ace Fabrics Limited

Unit 2 Boxwood Trading Estate, Kings Langley, HO3 2HT
Tel: (01234) 456789 Fax: (01234) 987654 E-mail: ace@fab.comp

To: *Miss Porter*   Date: *5 February 1999*[1]
        12 Elm Drive
        Milton Keynes
        ME9 427

This letter is to let you know that the terms or conditions of your contract have been amended as set out below.

If you wish to discuss any of these changes or require any further information, please let me know.

Date changes effective: *1 February 1999*

New wages/salary: *£15,000 per annum*

New hours of work: *8.30 am to 5.00 pm*

New location: *Wessex Trading Estate, High Wycombe*

Changes to duties and responsibilities: *none*

Please acknowledge receipt of this letter and your agreement to the terms set out in it by signing the attached copy of this letter and returning it to *Mr Smith*. You should retain the top copy with your contract of employment.

Signed:

....

for *Ace Fabrics Limited*

I, *Miss Porter*, acknowledge that I have received a statement of alteration to the particulars of my employment as required by the Employment Rights Act 1996 Section 1 and agree to the terms set out in that statement.

Signed: Dated:

Registered Office: Unit 2 Boxwood Trading Estate, Kings Langley, HO3 2HT
Registered in England no 123 4567

---

[1] This must be no later than one month after the change to the terms of employment.

Ace Fabrics Limited

Unit 2 Boxwood Trading Estate, Kings Langley, HO3 2HT
Tel: (01234) 456789 Fax: (01234) 987654 E-mail: ace@fab.comp

Dear *Jenny*,

I should like to express my congratulations to you on the birth of your baby.

I expect that you have now had time to consider your position. Therefore, I would like to know if you are still intending to return to work on or before *10 October 1999*.

Please respond to this letter within fourteen days, otherwise you will lose your legal right to return to work.

I look forward to hearing from you shortly, but if you have any queries please do not hesitate to contact me.

Yours sincerely

John Smith

John Smith
Personnel Manager

Registered Office: Unit 2 Boxwood Trading Estate, Kings Langley, HO3 2HT
Registered in England no 123 4567

---

[1] From 15th December 1999, the regulations on maternity change and this letter will no longer be valid.

EQUAL OPPORTUNITIES POLICY AT *ACE FABRICS LIMITED*

The Company's aim is to ensure that all of its employees and job applicants are treated equally irrespective of disability, race, colour, religion, nationality, ethnic origin, age, sex or marital status. This policy sets out instructions that all employees are required to follow in order to ensure that this is achieved.

Policy

1. There shall be no discrimination on account of disability, race, colour, religion, nationality, ethnic origin, age, sex or marital status.

2. The Company shall appoint, train, develop and promote on the basis of merit and ability.

3. Employees have personal responsibility for the practical application of the Company's Equal Opportunity Policy, which extends to the treatment of members of the public and employees.

4. Managers and supervisors who are involved in the recruitment, selection, promotion and training of employees have special responsibility for the practical application of the Company's Equal Opportunity Policy.

5. The Grievance Procedure[1] is available to any employee who believes that he or she may have been unfairly discriminated against.

6. Disciplinary action under the Disciplinary Procedure[2] shall be taken against any employee who is found to have committed an act of unlawful discrimination. Discriminatory conduct and sexual or racial harassment shall be regarded as gross misconduct.

7. If there is any doubt about appropriate treatment under the Company's Equal Opportunities Policy, employees should consult the Personnel Manager.[3]

---

[1] See Appendix 12.

[2] See Appendix 11.

[3] Employers may consider that a more detailed policy which may also incorporate a sexual and racial harassment policy, is more appropriate, in which case guidance should be obtained from the EOC, CRE or ACAS. See Appendix 30.

1. Employment tribunals

Employment tribunals (formerly 'industrial tribunals') determine applications relating to employment rights, the most important of which are the rights not to be unfairly dismissed; the right to a redundancy payment; the right not to be unlawfully discriminated against on grounds of sex, race or disability in relation to employment, and rights in relation to breaches of contract. The procedure is less formal than that of a court. Cases heard in tribunals may result in awards of compensation, reinstatement or re-engagement.

2. Employment Appeal Tribunal (EAT)

The EAT is a division of the High Court, presided over by a High Court judge. It hears appeals from the decisions of the employment tribunals on questions of law. Appeals from the EAT are to the Court of Appeal and from there to the House of Lords.

3. European Court of Justice

Where the decision of a case depends upon a question of European law and the answer to the question is not clear, the tribunal or court can refer the matter to the European Court of Justice.

4. Advisory Conciliation and Arbitration Service (ACAS)

ACAS was established by, and its activities are regulated by UK legislation.

The mission of ACAS is 'to improve the performance and effectiveness of organisations by providing an independent and impartial service to prevent and resolve disputes and to build harmonious relationships at work'. It provides advice to employers, employers associations, workers or trade unions on any matters concerned with the wide range of industrial relations services, including conciliation, arbitration, mediation and general and specific advice on industrial relations matters. ACAS may charge fees to those who benefit from the exercise of its functions. Fees are charged at present only for certain publications and seminars, and thus not for the key function of conciliation. ACAS also produces codes of practice and guidance on matters of industrial relations practice. Employment tribunals may take account of the provisions of such codes of practice when determining the fairness of a dismissal.

For addresses see Appendix 30.

APPENDIX 19
Capability Procedure
(for Responding to an Employee's Poor Performance)

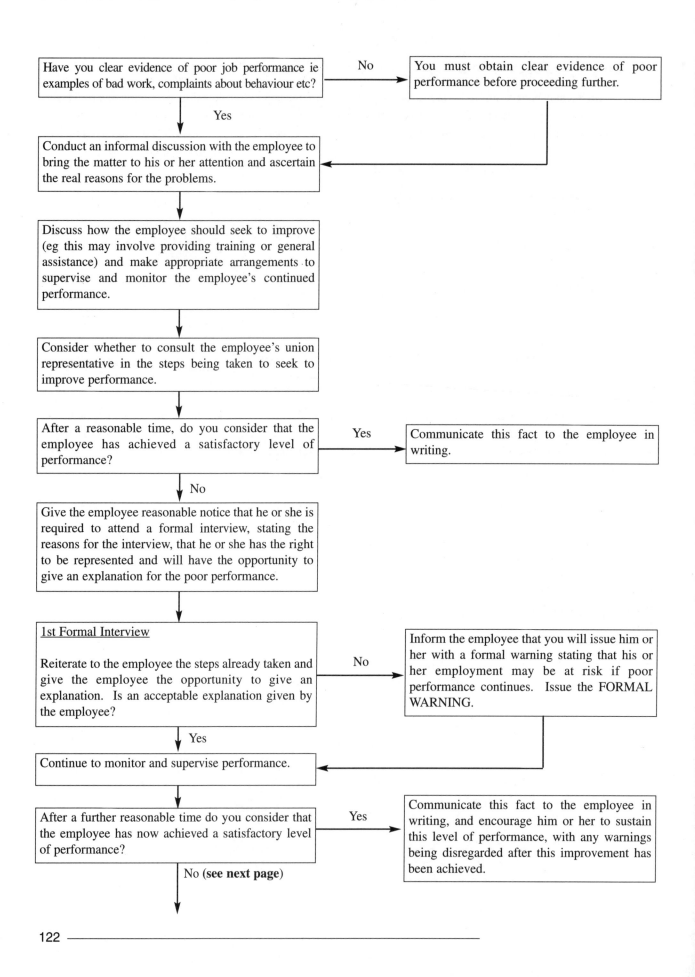

Have you clear evidence of poor job performance ie examples of bad work, complaints about behaviour etc?

No → You must obtain clear evidence of poor performance before proceeding further.

Yes

Conduct an informal discussion with the employee to bring the matter to his or her attention and ascertain the real reasons for the problems.

Discuss how the employee should seek to improve (eg this may involve providing training or general assistance) and make appropriate arrangements to supervise and monitor the employee's continued performance.

Consider whether to consult the employee's union representative in the steps being taken to seek to improve performance.

After a reasonable time, do you consider that the employee has achieved a satisfactory level of performance?

Yes → Communicate this fact to the employee in writing.

No

Give the employee reasonable notice that he or she is required to attend a formal interview, stating the reasons for the interview, that he or she has the right to be represented and will have the opportunity to give an explanation for the poor performance.

1st Formal Interview

Reiterate to the employee the steps already taken and give the employee the opportunity to give an explanation. Is an acceptable explanation given by the employee?

No → Inform the employee that you will issue him or her with a formal warning stating that his or her employment may be at risk if poor performance continues. Issue the FORMAL WARNING.

Yes

Continue to monitor and supervise performance.

After a further reasonable time do you consider that the employee has now achieved a satisfactory level of performance?

Yes → Communicate this fact to the employee in writing, and encourage him or her to sustain this level of performance, with any warnings being disregarded after this improvement has been achieved.

No (see next page)

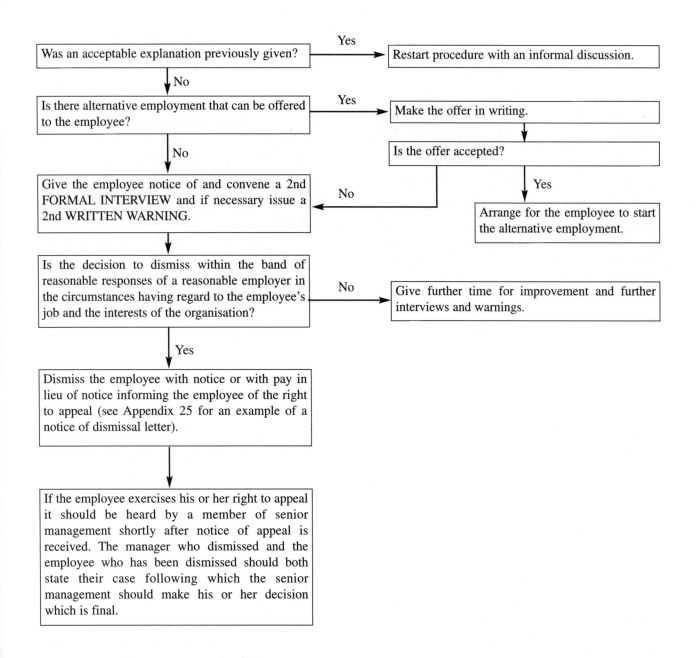

Was an acceptable explanation previously given? — Yes → Restart procedure with an informal discussion.

No ↓

Is there alternative employment that can be offered to the employee? — Yes → Make the offer in writing.

↓ Is the offer accepted?

No ↓

Give the employee notice of and convene a 2nd FORMAL INTERVIEW and if necessary issue a 2nd WRITTEN WARNING. ← No

Yes → Arrange for the employee to start the alternative employment.

Is the decision to dismiss within the band of reasonable responses of a reasonable employer in the circumstances having regard to the employee's job and the interests of the organisation? — No → Give further time for improvement and further interviews and warnings.

Yes ↓

Dismiss the employee with notice or with pay in lieu of notice informing the employee of the right to appeal (see Appendix 25 for an example of a notice of dismissal letter).

↓

If the employee exercises his or her right to appeal it should be heard by a member of senior management shortly after notice of appeal is received. The manager who dismissed and the employee who has been dismissed should both state their case following which the senior management should make his or her decision which is final.

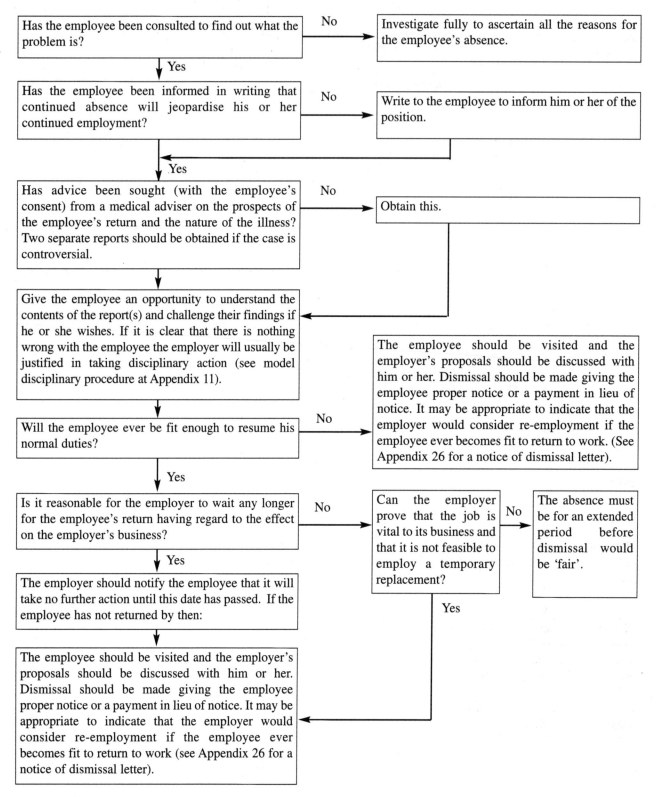

Note: This checklist is only a general guide and it should be remembered that each situation differs and the procedure may need to be adjusted to suit the circumstances.

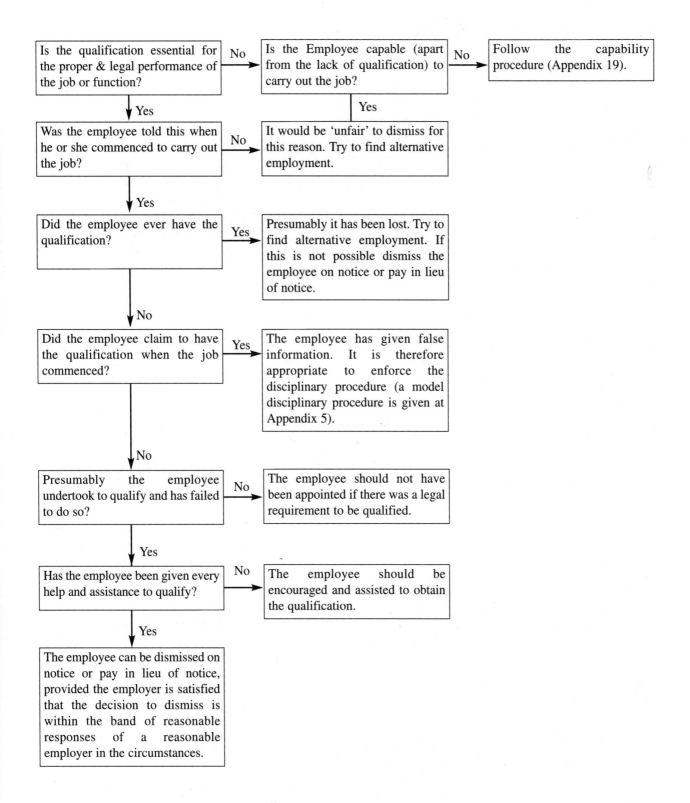

Is the qualification essential for the proper & legal performance of the job or function?

→ No → Is the Employee capable (apart from the lack of qualification) to carry out the job?

→ No → Follow the capability procedure (Appendix 19).

↓ Yes

Was the employee told this when he or she commenced to carry out the job?

→ No → It would be 'unfair' to dismiss for this reason. Try to find alternative employment.

(Yes from capability box ↓)

↓ Yes

Did the employee ever have the qualification?

→ Yes → Presumably it has been lost. Try to find alternative employment. If this is not possible dismiss the employee on notice or pay in lieu of notice.

↓ No

Did the employee claim to have the qualification when the job commenced?

→ Yes → The employee has given false information. It is therefore appropriate to enforce the disciplinary procedure (a model disciplinary procedure is given at Appendix 5).

↓ No

Presumably the employee undertook to qualify and has failed to do so?

→ No → The employee should not have been appointed if there was a legal requirement to be qualified.

↓ Yes

Has the employee been given every help and assistance to qualify?

→ No → The employee should be encouraged and assisted to obtain the qualification.

↓ Yes

The employee can be dismissed on notice or pay in lieu of notice, provided the employer is satisfied that the decision to dismiss is within the band of reasonable responses of a reasonable employer in the circumstances.

APPENDIX 22
Misconduct Procedures
(for Breach of the Employer's Disciplinary Rules)

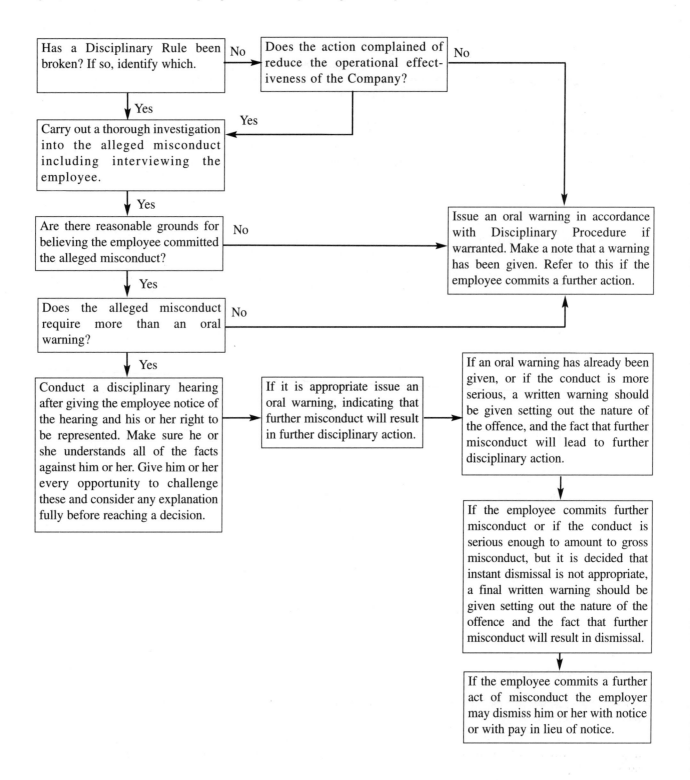

● If the misconduct was not committed at work, dismissal can only be effected if the action complained of has a direct bearing on the employee's job.

● The appropriate Procedure will vary according to the facts of each case and the above procedure should only be used as an outline rather than as standard procedure.

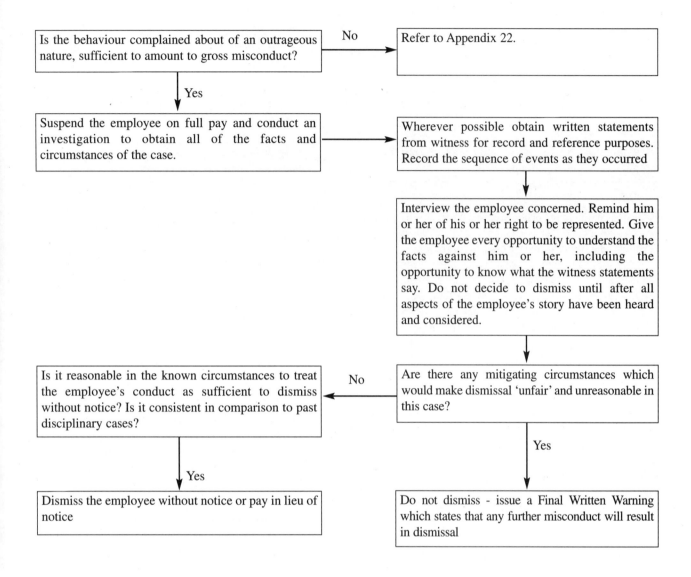

● If the misconduct was not committed at work, dismissal can only be effected if the misconduct has a direct bearing on the employee's job.

● For dismissal without notice to occur it is essential to ensure that the action complained of is sufficient in its own right to justify this severe action. Dismissals which follow warnings must be carried out with either notice or pay in lieu of notice.

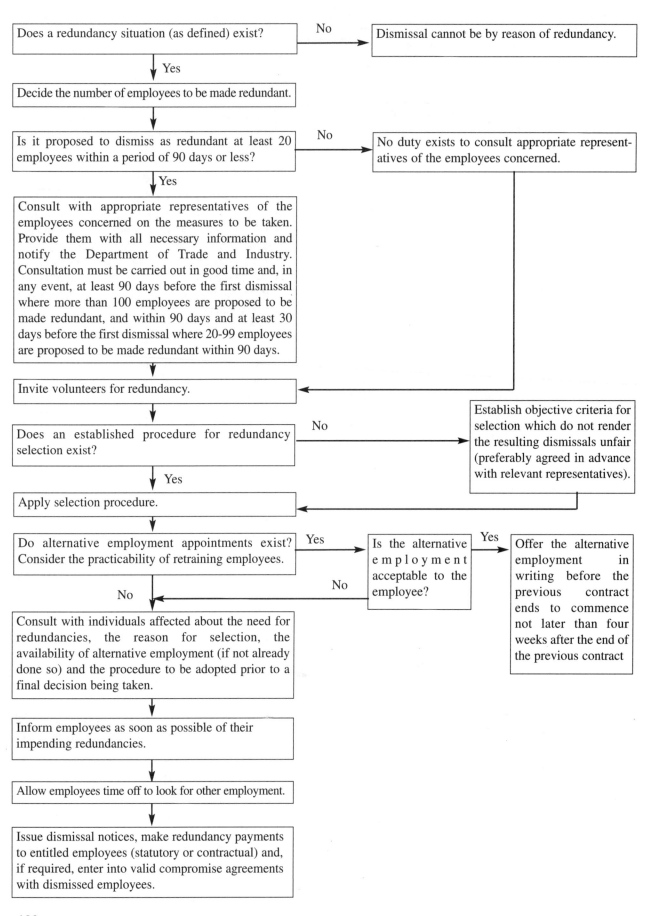

Does a redundancy situation (as defined) exist? — No → Dismissal cannot be by reason of redundancy.

↓ Yes

Decide the number of employees to be made redundant.

↓

Is it proposed to dismiss as redundant at least 20 employees within a period of 90 days or less? — No → No duty exists to consult appropriate representatives of the employees concerned.

↓ Yes

Consult with appropriate representatives of the employees concerned on the measures to be taken. Provide them with all necessary information and notify the Department of Trade and Industry. Consultation must be carried out in good time and, in any event, at least 90 days before the first dismissal where more than 100 employees are proposed to be made redundant, and within 90 days and at least 30 days before the first dismissal where 20-99 employees are proposed to be made redundant within 90 days.

↓

Invite volunteers for redundancy. ←

↓

Does an established procedure for redundancy selection exist? — No → Establish objective criteria for selection which do not render the resulting dismissals unfair (preferably agreed in advance with relevant representatives).

↓ Yes

Apply selection procedure. ←

↓

Do alternative employment appointments exist? Consider the practicability of retraining employees. — Yes → Is the alternative employment acceptable to the employee? — Yes → Offer the alternative employment in writing before the previous contract ends to commence not later than four weeks after the end of the previous contract

No ← ← No

Consult with individuals affected about the need for redundancies, the reason for selection, the availability of alternative employment (if not already done so) and the procedure to be adopted prior to a final decision being taken.

↓

Inform employees as soon as possible of their impending redundancies.

↓

Allow employees time off to look for other employment.

↓

Issue dismissal notices, make redundancy payments to entitled employees (statutory or contractual) and, if required, enter into valid compromise agreements with dismissed employees.

Ace Fabrics Limited

Unit 2 Boxwood Trading Estate, Kings Langley, HO3 2HT
Tel: (01234) 456789 Fax: (01234) 987654 E-mail: ace@fab.comp

Dear *Miss Porter*,

I refer to our meeting on *15 July 1999*.

As I explained at the meeting, you have been unable to carry out your duties to the standards required by the Company. Therefore, we have no alternative but to terminate your employment with the Company with effect from *15 August 1999*.

As you are aware, we have provided you with training and assistance to enable you to improve your performance but without success. In addition, we have attempted to find suitable alternative employment within the Company, but regret that nothing is available.

You are entitled to be paid in full, including any accrued holiday pay, during your notice period.

I take this opportunity of reminding you that you are entitled to appeal against this decision through the Company's disciplinary procedure. If you wish to exercise this right you must let me know within two working days of receipt of this letter.

It is with regret that we have had to take this action. We should like to thank you for your past efforts for the Company and wish you every success for the future.

Yours sincerely

John Smith

John Smith
Personnel Manager

Registered Office: Unit 2 Boxwood Trading Estate, Kings Langley, HO3 2HT
Registered in England no 123 4567

Ace Fabrics Limited

Unit 2 Boxwood Trading Estate, Kings Langley, HO3 2HT
Tel: (01234) 456789 Fax: (01234) 987654 E-mail: ace@fab.comp

Dear *Miss Porter,*

I refer to our meeting at your home on *18 July 1999.*

I was very sorry to hear that your condition has not improved and that it is unlikely that you will be able to resume working.

As we discussed, there is little we can do to assist your return to work and our medical adviser has reported that you are not likely to be well enough to return to your current job for some time, if at all. We have tried to find some alternative suitable work for you but, as you know, all of the work in this Company is fairly heavy work and there is nothing we can offer you.

I regret that I have no alternative other than to give you notice to terminate your employment with the Company with effect from *22 August 1999.*

You are entitled to full pay for the period of your notice plus accrued holiday pay. I shall arrange for these sums to be paid to you, and for your P45 to be sent to you as soon as possible.

If your health does improve in the future to enable you to resume working, I would be pleased to discuss re-employing you.

Yours sincerely

John Smith

John Smith
Personnel Manager

Registered Office: Unit 2 Boxwood Trading Estate, Kings Langley, HO3 2HT
Registered in England no 123 4567

---

[1] This letter is an example of dismissal due to terminal illness. Such a letter would have to be re-worded if the employee was likely to be able to resume work at some future date.

Ace Fabrics Limited
Unit 2 Boxwood Trading Estate, Kings Langley, HO3 2HT
Tel: (01234) 456789 Fax: (01234) 987654 E-mail: ace@fab.comp

Dear *Miss Porter,*

It is with regret that I write to inform you that the Company had decided to make you redundant with effect from today. You are aware that the Company is being restructured and the volume of work has substantially diminished.

We have tried to find you a suitable position commensurate with your abilities elsewhere within the Company but there is nothing available.

You are entitled to *one month's* notice of termination but we believe it is better for you and all others concerned if you leave immediately. The Company will pay you a gross sum of *£1223.39* as compensation for the termination of your employment subject to such deductions as the Company is required to make from the sum in respect of any tax charges or levies. This sum is calculated as follows:

    (a)   *4 weeks' gross salary at £13,500 per annum*   *£1038.46*

    (b)   *5 days* accrued holiday   *£184.93*

In addition, the Company will make you a statutory redundancy payment of *£990*. This is calculated in accordance with your age, salary (subject to a statutory maximum of £220 per week) and the number of years service with the Company.

    i.e.   *$1\frac{1}{2}$ x £220 x 3*

1.   The Company will therefore pay you a total sum of *£2213.39* immediately on your signature and return of the enclosed copy of this letter.

2.   You accept that this payment made by the Company is in full and final settlement of your claim for compensation and/or damages for the termination of your employment with effect from today.[1]

3.   You will return all property in your possession belonging to the Company.

continued...

Registered Office: Unit 2 Boxwood Trading Estate, Kings Langley, HO3 2HT
Registered in England no 123 4567

---

[1] Note that a compromise agreement is needed to refrain the employee from bringing proceedings in an employment tribunal (see Appendices 28 & 29).

Please acknowledge receipt of this letter by signing and returning the acknowledgement on the enclosed copy of this letter.

Yours sincerely

John Smith

John Smith
Personnel Manager

I acknowledge receipt of the letter of which the above is a copy and of the compensation payment referred to in it.

Signed ....

Date of Signature

Ace Fabrics Limited

Unit 2 Boxwood Trading Estate, Kings Langley, HO3 2HT
Tel: (01234) 456789 Fax: (01234) 987654 E-mail: ace@fab.comp

Dear *Miss Porter,*

I hereby confirm the terms we have agreed in relation to the termination of your employment with *Ace Fabrics Limited* ("the Company") with effect from *26 July 1999*

1.   The Company will make you an ex gratia payment of *£2,000* payable immediately on your return of the enclosed copy of this letter.

2.   You agree to refrain from initiating any proceedings before an Employment Tribunal alleging that the Company *dismissed you unfairly, discriminated against you on the grounds of race, sex or disability or has made an unlawful deduction from your wages and to withdraw any such proceedings now in progress.*[1]

3.   You accept that this payment made by the Company is in full and final settlement of all claims of any kind which you are or might be entitled to make against the Company, its officers, shareholders or employees in connection with your employment or its termination, including any claims which are now proceeding before an Industrial Tribunal.

4.   You will return all property in your possession belonging to the Company on or before *1 August 1999.*

5.   You agree to pay any tax due in respect of the sums referred to above or to reimburse the Company for any tax the Company is required to pay in respect of such sums.

6.   You agree to keep the terms of this agreement confidential.

continued...

Registered Office: Unit 2 Boxwood Trading Estate, Kings Langley, HO3 2HT
Registered in England no 123 4567

[1] These are just examples; you should only include those matters over which there may be a real risk of a valid claim from an individual.

7. We hereby state that, the conditions regulating this agreement under [Section 203 of the Employment Rights Act 1996, under Section 77 of the Sex Discrimination Act 1975, under Section 72 of the Race Relations Act 1996 and under Section 9 of the Disability Discrimination Act 1995] [2] are satisfied. You, in turn, acknowledge and understand that you are required to take independent legal advice from a qualified lawyer on the terms and effect of this agreement. The qualified lawyer who provides you with independent legal advice is required to sign the acknowledgement on the enclosed copy of this letter.

Please signify your acceptance of the above by signing and returning the acknowledgement on the enclosed copy of this letter.

Yours sincerely

John Smith

John Smith
Personnel Manager

---

[2] Include relevant Act(s) as appropriate.

Acknowledgement

I acknowledge receipt of the letter of which the above is a copy and of the sum of *£2,000* referred to in it.

I confirm that I have taken independent advice from *John Black of Black & Brown Solicitor of 2 High Street, Maidenhead, Berkshire* and I confirm and agree to the terms set out in the letter.

Signed ....

Date of Signature:

I *John Black* of *Black & Brown Solicitors* confirm that *Miss Porter* has received independent legal advice within the meaning of Section 203(4) of the Employment Rights Act 1996 as to the terms and effect of this terms of the letter of which the above is a copy and in particular its effect on her ability to pursue her rights before an industrial tribunal. I am, and was at the time I gave the advice referred to, a Solicitor of the Supreme Court, holding a current practising certificate and there is, and was at the time I gave the advice, in force a policy of insurance covering the risk of a claim by *Miss Porter* in respect of any loss arising in consequent of the advice I gave.[1]

Signed ....

[1] The Employment Rights (Dispute Resolution) Act 1998 increases the number of people qualified to give relevant independent advice for the purposes of concluding valid compromise agreements. In addition to qualified lawyers, officers (or officials, employees or members) of an independent trade union and workers at advice centres (such as Citizens Advice Bureaux) can now sign compromise agreements. However they must still be covered by a policy of insurance or an indemnity against negligent advice provided by a professional body. If this occurs the letter should be amended accordingly.

Ace Fabrics Limited

Unit 2 Boxwood Trading Estate, Kings Langley, HO3 2HT
Tel: (01234) 456789 Fax: (01234) 987654 Email:ace@fab.comp

Dear *Miss Porter,*

It is with regret that I write to inform you that the Company has decided to make you redundant with effect from *26 July 1999.* You are aware of and we have discussed the reasons for your redundancy.

We have tried to find you a suitable position commensurate with your abilities elsewhere within the Company but there is nothing available.

The Company has however decided to make you an ex gratia payment of *£2,000* as compensation for the termination of your employment. In addition, the Company will make you a statutory redundancy payment of *£945.*

The statutory redundancy payment is calculated in accordance with your age, salary (subject to a statutory maximum of £220 per week) and the number of years service with the Company.

i.e. $1\frac{1}{2}$ x £220 x 3

1.   The Company will therefore pay you a total sum of *£2,990* payable immediately on your return of the enclosed copy of this letter.

2.   You agree to refrain from initiating any proceedings before an Employment Tribunal alleging that the Company has *dismissed you unfairly, discriminated against you on the grounds of race, sex or disability or has made an unlawful deduction from your wages, and to withdraw any such proceedings now in progress.*[1]

3.   You accept that this payment made by the Company is in full and final settlement of all claims of any kind which you are or might be entitled to make against the Company, its officers, shareholders or employees in connection with your employment or its termination including any claims which are now proceeding before an Employment Tribunal.

4.   You will return all property in your possession belonging to the Company on or before *1 August 1998.*

5.   You agree to pay any tax due in respect of the sums referred to above or to reimburse the Company for any tax the Company is required to pay in respect of such sums.

continued...

Registered Office: Unit 2 Boxwood Trading Estate, Kings Langley, HO3 2HT
Registered in England no 123 4567

[1] These are just examples; you should only include those matters over which there may be a real risk of a valid claim from an individual.

6. You agree to keep the terms of this agreement confidential.

7. We hereby state that, the conditions regulating this agreement under [Section 203 of the Employment Rights Act 1996, under Section 77 of the Sex Discrimination Act 1975, under Section 72 of the Race Relations Act 1996 and under Section 9 of the Disability Discrimination Act 1995] [2] are satisfied. You, in turn, acknowledge and understand that you are required to take independent legal advice from a qualified lawyer on the terms and effect of this agreement. The qualified lawyer who provides you with independent legal advice is required to sign the acknowledgement on the enclosed copy of this letter.

Please signify your acceptance of the above by signing and returning the acknowledgement on the enclosed copy of this letter.

Yours sincerely

John Smith

John Smith
Personnel Manager

---

[2] Include relevant Act(s) as appropriate.

Acknowledgement

I acknowledge receipt of the letter of which the above is a copy and of the sum of £2,990 referred to in it.

I confirm that I have taken independent advice from *John Black of Black & Brown Solicitors of 2 High Street, Maidenhead, Berkshire* and I confirm and agree to the terms set out in the letter.

Signed ....

Date of Signature:

I *John Black* of *Black & Brown Solicitors* confirm that *Miss Porter* has received independent legal advice within the meaning of Section 203(4) of the Employment Rights Act 1996 as to the terms and effect of this terms of the letter of which the above is a copy and in particular its effect on her ability to pursue her rights before an industrial tribunal. I am, and was at the time I gave the advice referred to, a Solicitor of the Supreme Court, holding a current practising certificate and there is, and was at the time I gave the advice, in force a policy of insurance covering the risk of a claim by *Miss Porter* in respect of any loss arising in consequent of the advice I gave.[1]

Signed ....

[1] The Employment Rights (Dispute Resolution) Act 1998 increases the number of people qualified to give relevant independent advice for the purposes of concluding valid compromise agreements. In addition to qualified lawyers, officers (or officials, employees or members) of an independent trade union and workers at advice centres (such as Citizens Advice Bureaux) can now sign compromise agreements. However they must still be covered by a policy of insurance or an indemnity against negligent advice provided by a professional body. If this occurs the letter should be amended accordingly.

Advisory Conciliation and Arbitration Service (ACAS)
Head Office   Tel: 020 7210 3000
Brandon House
180 Borough High Street
London SE1 1LW

Commission for Racial Equality (CRE)
Head Office   Tel: 020 728 7022
Elliot House   E-mail: info@cre.gov.uk
10-12 Allington Street   Web site: www.cre.gov.uk
London SW1E 5EH

Data Protection Registrar
Wycliffe House   Tel: 01625 545745
Waber Lane   E-mail: data@wycliffe.demon.co.uk
Wilmslow SK9 5AX   Web site: www.open.gov.uk/dpr/dprhome/htm

Department for Education and Employment
Carton House   Tel: 020 7925 5000
Tothill Street   Web site: www.dfee.gov.uk
London SW1H 9NF

Department for Education and Employment
Overseas Labour Service
W5 Moorfoot   Tel: 0114 259 4074
Sheffield S1 4PQ   Web site: www.dfee.gov.uk/ols

Department of Trade and Industry
1 Victoria Street   Tel: 020 7215 5000
London SW1H 0ET   Web site: www.dti.gov.uk

Employment Appeal Tribunal
Audit House   Tel: 020 7273 1041
58 Victoria Embankment
London EC4Y 0DS

Employment Service
Level 6 Caxton House   Tel: 020 7273 6111
Tothill Street   Web site: www.employmentservice.gov.uk
London SW1H 9NE

Employment Tribunal Central Enquiries
100 Southgate Street   Tel: 0345 959775
Bury St Edmunds IP33 2AQ   Web site: www.dti.gov.uk/index.html

Equal Opportunities Commission
Overseas House   Tel: 0161 833 9244
Quay Street   Web site: www.eoc.org.uk/index.html
Manchester M3 3HN

European Commission
8 Storey's Gate   Tel: 020 7973 1992
London SW1P 3AT   www.cec.org.uk

European Court of Justice

Palais de la Cour de Justice   Tel: 00 352 4303 1
Boulevard Konrad Adenauer   Web site: www.curia.eu.int
Kirchberg
L-2925
Luxembourg

Health and Safety Executive Commission

Head Office   Tel: 020 7717 6000 (Infoline 0541 545 500)
Rose Court   Web site: www.open.gov.uk/hse/hsehome.htm
2 Southwark Bridge
London SE1 9HS

Health and Safety Executive Books

PO Box 1999   Tel: 01787 881165
Sudbury   Web site: www.open.gov.uk/hse/hsehome.htm
Suffolk CO10 6FS

National Disability Council

The Adelphi
1-11 John Adam Street
London WC2N 6HT

National Minimum Wage Helpline

Tel: 0845 6000 678

Race Relations Employment Advisory Service

14th Floor Cumberland House   Tel: 0121 244 8141/2/3
200 Broad Street   Email: hqrreas@dfee.gov.uk
Birmingham B14 1TA

Index